IN HEAVEN!
EXPERIENCING THE
THRONE OF GOD

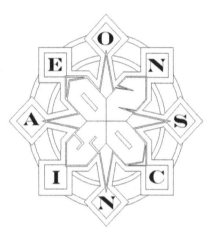

Dean Braxton

But even if we, or an angel from heaven, preach any
other gospel to you than what we have preached
to you, let him be accursed. - Gal 1:8

In Heaven! Experiencing the Throne of God
by Dean Braxton

Printed in the United States of America

ISBN 9781615790678

Unless otherwise indicated, Bible quotations are taken from
The New King James Version of the Bible. Copyright © 1982
by Thomas Nelson.

www.xulonpress.com

Comments

❖

Dean is the first, to my knowledge, to balance his approach. He, of course, knows what he saw and knows it to be real and true. But, Dean has not chosen to abandon his basic belief that the Word of God is even more real than any supernatural experience, as the Apostle Peter addressed in 2 Peter 1:16-21. This will be a life changing and revelatory work, without requiring us to compromise our belief in the veracity of the Bible.

Pastor Don Ricci
Pastor of World Outreach Center – Boise, Idaho.

I have heard Dean Braxton's testimony and have spent time with him, and it is very evident that he has been with Jesus. Audiences have asked him hundreds of questions, and his answers always give insight from Heaven. He shares his testimony to draw people to Jesus, and not to himself. As you read this book, hear with your heart, and allow the presence of the Lord to change your life!

By His Excellency,
Bishop Donald R. Kennedy
Holy Apostolic Catholic Church, order of St. Thomas

In getting to know Dean and Marilyn Braxton, I have found in them a true and sincere Christian faith. Having traveled with Dean in South America, I found in him a true desire that people of all strata of society know that Heaven does exist and that God truly loves them and wants them to be there with Him forever. My desire is that the reading of this book will inspire you to seek your Creator and to find in Him rest for your soul and hope for this present life on Earth. And, most importantly, to know that there is hope for you in Eternity.

Rick Daviscourt - President
Restoring Hope International

Dean's testimony has increased my faith, of which I am grateful. No man could have thought of the things I have heard him say. It is not so much than my head understands what he says, but it is my spirit that leaps inside me that makes me rejoice when I hear his experience.

Rusty and Catherine Roberson,
Facilities Maintenance Manager, Teacher
By His Word Christian Center – Tacoma, Wa

I too, like so many others, have heard and believe this powerful life changing experience, that Dean Braxton shared. It was so beautiful and came at a time that ended up being a confirmation for me. At the time, my mother was dying and I had questions about Heaven. Dean set my soul at ease, with his message of hope, beauty and peace.

Carolyn Williams, Probation Counselor,
King County Superior Court
New Covenant Church – Seattle, Washington

Dean and I have been close friends for the past twenty three years. I can best describe him and his wife, Marilyn, as having a burning passion to bring others into the Kingdom of God, and encourage those who have already joined by the mercy and grace of God. They build relationships with people by giving of themselves.

Randy Barnett
Emmanuel Church at Embassy Center of Bremerton, WA

I knew Dean Braxton and his family before his heaven experience. We went to church and Bible studies together. His testimony of going to heaven and meeting Jesus has given me a new perspective on life and my eventual death. People who have passed on before me are in heaven now singing praises to Jesus and I will see them when my time on earth is done.

Jon Febus, Senior Process Engineer
Joy of Life Church - Puyallup, WA

After listining to Dean's account it dawned on me that the thing that most of the other accounts were missing was "Scripture"... They were fabulous stories with no Scripture to back them up. That is not the case with Dean's testimony. Dean has Scripture after Scripture confirming what he experienced. I would say, sit down with a Bible in hand and look up the Scriptures as you read this book, and open your heart and allow the Holy Spirit to guide you into all truth.

Bob Bennett Music Minister
Sound from Heaven Church, Stanwood WA

Dean's testimony has sparked my heart to new things about my Father. Sometimes we get so focused on the daily issues that we lose sight of how much the Father loves us and He sees things from beginning to end. Dean's testimony is shared through the Word of God.

Bryan Huffman, Lead Gutter Installer
By His Word Christian Center – Tacoma, Washington

I have known Dean and Marilyn for a couple of years. They are solid down to earth people. They have their feet planted on the Rock, Christ Jesus and know who they are in God. They know how to take their authority and speak into peoples lives. They know how to take the horns of the alter till they hear from heaven. They both have a heart after God for people.
Pamela J. Sharp
By His Word Christian Center – Tacoma, WA

Dean Braxton gives the modern Church a glimpse into an eternal place that few get to see and then return and tell. The things he has seen and describes are scriptural and incredibly challenging to those who have their mind made up about what lies beyond. The eternal connection of families and Divine strategies being planned on our behalf are exciting and comforting.
Pastor Brian J. Cuff, Senior Pastor
Church of the Harvest – Eugene, Oregon

I discovered a man of integrity that wanted to be able to support all he shared openly with the Word of God. I have met very few individuals in my life that have had a miraculous experience and push and direct the attention away from themselves and back to God and His Precious Son Jesus that, as Dean repeats many times ''DESERVES ALL THE GLORY'' because He did this for us!
Aaron Kroeger, Owner - Stephens Automatic Door Co. Inc.
By His Word Christian Center – Tacoma, Washington

I met Dean and his wife Marilyn three years ago when he came to minister at St. Luke's in Seattle, WA. I immediately 'connected' with Dean as he shared with me privately before the service about his amazing experiences in heaven.

Reading this testimony will help to bring peace to your heart and will answer some of the questions you may have had about the place we as Christians call 'home.' As amazing as his testimony is, the faith of his wife Marilyn throughout this ordeal is a story in and of itself! Her unswerving faith and tenacious pursuit of God's promises during this season will encourage all of us who are standing in faith for a loved one.

Dr. Bruce & Reshma Allen
Still Waters International Ministries - Chewelah, WA

Contents

꿈

Foreward

❧

There are a lot of things about Heaven in the Bible but we haven't understood them because we didn't know that is what it is talking about. Once you have read this book, many of your questions will have been answered as mine were.

I have been serving the Lord for well over 60 years and have always had a hunger to know what Heaven is really like so God brought Dean and Marilyn Braxton into my life to give me a firsthand view of what it's like.

It was in 2007 that I met Dean at a Friday night Bible Study where he had been invited to share his experience of dying and going to Heaven and coming back. Marilyn shared what was going on with struggles on this earth at the hospital and Dean shared what was going on in Heaven and the first thing he found out was that his spirit instantly knew where to go. Thank God our citizenship is in Heaven! We go Home!

Shortly after that, Pastor Butler invited Dean and Marilyn to come to our church and share their testimony and because of that Pastor, Dean and I have spent many hours talking about his experience and how it fits the Word of God. What a wonderful and glorious life we have to look forward to!

While Dean was in Heaven for an hour and forty five minutes, the Lord showed him many things and downloaded into his spirit so much information that two things happened.

One, was that he didn't want to come back to the earth - who would? The other was that he knew he needed to verify everything he saw there in the Word of God.

So my friend, as you read this book you will be encouraged, blessed and strengthened to be "strong in the Lord and in the power of His might." I trust that this book will also encourage you to become a soul winner. By the signs we see all around us our Lord is coming back soon.

Your Brother in Christ,
John Cook, Assistant Pastor
By His Word Christian Center – Tacoma, WA

Introduction

❧

Over the years, I've never been impressed with heavenly experiences in people's lives. For when those who have claimed to have them, I could never really validate them with the Word of God.

About two years ago, my assistant in the ministry introduced me to Dean Braxton's experience of going to heaven. After listening to his experience and bearing witness in my spirit, the Lord spoke to me to have him come and share with our church. From that moment on, Dean and his lovely wife, Marilyn, have remained with us ever since.

I really feel blessed having Dean's experience in my life for the tremendous witness to so many scriptures, even to the point of revealing the understanding of passages that we never had the insight before.

So take the journey with Dean as he connects scripture to every account of his experience and be blessed!

Jann T. Butler, Senior Pastor
By His Word Christian Center – Tacoma, WA

Chapter 1

"No, It Is Not Your Time"

꒰❀꒱

W hat I do remember, is the first time I was before Jesus
He said, *"No, It is not your time. Go back."* I seemed
to be OK with that. So I left to come back to earth. I got to
what I would call the edge of heaven, and knew that my
body was not ready. I cannot tell you how or why I knew, I
just knew. On returning back to the feet of Jesus, I saw a lot
of different things throughout heaven. I also communicated
to a number of beings. I call them BEINGS because they
were BEING everything God had created them to be.

When I reached Jesus the second time, He said, *"No, It
is not your time. Go back."* The second time He told me to
go back was a little more firm, and I cried on the inside. So
I left again. When I reached the edge of heaven, this time, I
experienced something that does not bring happiness.

At the edge of heaven is thick darkness - a blackness
like you have never experienced here on earth. You could
hold it in your hands if you wanted to. I do not think our
physical body could penetrate it. It was that thick. I had to
pass through it to get to heaven, and later, when I left heaven
to return back to earth, I went through it again. I knew it was
filled with demons. But, when I passed through this black-

ness, no demon could touch me because I was a child of God. I did not experience any fear going through it to heaven, or when I left to come back to earth.

This second time I reached the edge of heaven, I heard the cries of those who were in hell. I heard the screams, the shrieks, the screeches, the squeals, and the yells of pain from hell of fallen creations (people) of God. I knew if I looked over, I would see what was happening to them there. But I just did not have any desire to look. It was not Jesus' will for any human to be there. Since it was not his will, I had no will to look. Just to think about this always brings a great sadness inside of me. It brings me no happiness talking about it, as I said before. Again, I traveled through parts of heaven and communicated to more of God's creations as I returned to Jesus' feet.

The third time I was before Him, He said, *"NO, IT IS NOT YOUR TIME. GO BACK!"* When he said to go back this time, He was more stern. When He said it the third time, I cried like a baby on the inside. These are the only words He spoke to me. Another way He communicated to me, besides saying, "Go back" in words I could hear, was that He would just look at me and put information into me that He wanted me to know. The same way a computer receives information. I just remember looking into His eyes as He downloaded all kinds of information into me. I continue to experience and acquire new information and insights. I am discovering new ways to explain what I saw. I understand things in the Holy Bible as I have never understood them before. Even as I am writing this, there are new revelations that arise for me, that I will put in this explanation of what happened to me.

The Pain In My Side

At the time this happened, I was the Program Manager for two King County Superior Juvenile Courts in Seattle, Washington. One court works with juveniles who are chemically dependent (Drug Court), and the other works with juveniles that are mentally ill (Treatment Court). This day just happened to be my Drug Court day. On mornings before a court hearing, a team of us would discuss the youth in the court to see how they are doing. On the team is a judge, the judge's bailiff, a staff from detention, a prosecuting attorney, a defense attorney, a police officer, an educator, a mental health counselor, a chemical dependency counselor, two juvenile probation counselors, and myself as the manager.

On Thursday May 4th, 2006, I was driving to work, knowing that the pain in my side, this time, would not go away as easily as it had in the past. But, I believed if I could get to work and lay on the floor, the pain would go away. When I arrived at work at 7 AM, I went to the bathroom and believed the pain would go away after relieving myself, but it did not. After I arrived at my office, I laid on the floor and still, the pain did not go away. This time, I knew the pain would not go away. I had the pain before, and knew it was kidneys stones. I was thinking I would pass them and the pain would stop. However, this time, something was wrong. I decided that I needed to go back home. I left the building and informed the security guard at the entry door that I was heading home, and asked him if he would let my staff know I was leaving, and he said he would. He asked me what was wrong. I told him, "Kidney stones," and that I would be OK. Out in the parking lot, I ran into a co-worker and asked her to take the snacks for the staff meeting before court, because I was leaving.

On My Way To The Hospital

The drive back home was 45 minutes to an hour. On the way home, I vomited a number of times in the car. When I arrived home, I was in a lot of pain and laid down on the hard floor hoping this would relieve the pain, but it did not, and so off to the emergency room (ER) I went. When I entered the

ER at the hospital, I was doubled over and let the staff know I believed I was in pain because of kidney stones. They took me right into a room and gave me some pain medication. I was not used to taking medications. I could not remember taking any sick days in the past three years. My wife, Marilyn, showed up and talked with the doctor about the problem. The doctor confirmed that I had numerous kidney stones with one stuck high on the right side and it was causing all the problems. The doctor also came up with a plan to operate the next day and wanted me to stay overnight. What they do with most kidney stones, is use a machine that uses ultra sonic waves (ultra sound) to break them up so you can pass them easier. It just so happened, that the machine would be at that hospital the next day. They wanted me to stay in the hospital overnight and to have the stones broken up using this machine the next day.

A Simple Operation

Marilyn had to deal with not only me being in the hospital, but we were supposed to have left that night to visit family in Texas and come back with our son, Gabriel, who was attending Christ for the Nations Bible College. Marilyn, with a friend, got our flight changed to May 8th. So, everything was set, it was supposed to be a simple operation, and out the next day. That is what I had believed would happen, because I had this operation four years ago and checked in one morning and was out that afternoon.

After I came to, seven days later, I was in the Intensive Care Unit (ICU) at another hospital, and I was wondering, "what happened!" (Later, in this book my wife will give you her account on what happened during that time.) All I can remember is that after the operation, they were trying to give me oxygen and I could not breathe. Then, they wanted to put a pic-line in me and I signed a paper to OK the procedure.

Seven days later, they took the breathing tube out of my mouth and I looked at my parents and older brother and told them I had seen Jesus three times. I knew I had died and was prayed back to life by many people who believed Jesus would heal me. Later, I had found out they did CPR on me for an hour and 45 minutes. How long I was with Jesus, I cannot tell you. It seemed long and it seemed short. I know EVERYTHING – IS - RIGHT, where Jesus is, and THERE IS NOTHING WRONG! Some say it is peaceful, but it far exceeds past peace because there is nothing to be peaceful from. When I first arrived in heaven and knelt before Jesus, all I could do was say, "YOU DID THIS FOR ME?!! THANK YOU, THANK YOU, THANK YOU, THANK YOU, THANK YOU, and THANK YOU!!" I could have said this for the next 3000 years or more and still would have wanted to keep going. Jesus is bright and we that are RIGHT with Him can look at Him. He is brighter than the noonday sun, but we can still look at Him, if you are RIGHT with Him. There is more I can tell you, but that will have to wait for now.

All I can end with now is that: EVERYTHING – WAS – RIGHT!! - in heaven.

Chapter 2

I Am Just A Man

᭬

Before we go any further in this book I want everyone who reads this book to know I am just a man. I was not sent back with any super hero power. I have the same Holy Spirit in me that every one of us who has asked Jesus to be their Lord and Savior has. I've had others try to treat me special because of what happened to me. I've even heard others say I was lucky or blessed to go to heaven and come back, to see Jesus and God the Father. I must let everyone know that I was sent back to do the same thing that all of us that accept Jesus into our lives as Lord and Savior, are supposed to do. That is to tell people about Jesus and how He loves them and has a place for them for all of eternity. I am no different than anyone who loves Jesus.

Now, to understand how I look at people who have not gone through this experience, you must read about a man named Thomas in the book of John.

John 20:24-29 (NKJV)
Now Thomas, called the Twin, one of the twelve, was not with them when Jesus came. The other disciples therefore said to him, "We have seen the

Lord." So he said to them, "Unless I see in His hands the print of the nails, and put my finger into the print of the nails, and put my hand into His side, I will not believe." And after eight days His disciples were again inside, and Thomas with them. Jesus came, the doors being shut, and stood in the midst, and said, "Peace to you!" Then He said to Thomas, "Reach your finger here, and look at My hands; and reach your hand here, and put it into My side. Do not be unbelieving, but believing." And Thomas answered and said to Him, "My Lord and my God!" Jesus said to him, "Thomas, because you have seen Me, you have believed. Blessed are those who have not seen and yet have believed."

In this story of Thomas you read that AFTER he saw Jesus he believed, and Jesus said back to him, *"Thomas, because you have seen Me, you have believed. Blessed are those who have not seen and yet have believed."* I look at everyone who has not seen Jesus as I have seen Him as blessed because Jesus said so. So as you read on, understand - you that know Jesus as Lord and Savior, you are blessed, blessed, and blessed.

We all have the same job to accomplish here on earth and that is to tell as many people as we can about our Lord and Savior Jesus Christ.

What Really Matters Is That You Are There!

The other area I want to go over is that if you do not believe me that is OK. The most important thing is that you go to heaven. When you get there you will see. It wouldn't even matter if I am right. What will matter, is that you are there!

I have come to understand that it really is not I who gets a person in heaven or keeps them out. It really is not anyone here on earth. It is Jesus. Really, it is all about Him, and because of that understanding, I do not have to perform to get in heaven, and you do not have to perform either. I know a person who is approved of God will want to serve Him because they love Him, not for what it will get them. I know they will proclaim His name to all because of the love they have for Him. They will walk in His ways because of the love they have for Him.

So again, if after reading this book, you have a hard time believing what I have written, that is OK. Many of the things I write about won't get you in or keep you out. Many of the thoughts we fight about in our believing in God won't change whether we are going to heaven or not. I do believe it stops us from being a more effective witness for Jesus, but it will not keep us from entering heaven. He really is looking at your heart. There are many people in heaven whom I did not think would make it but did, and many whom I believed would make it but did not. Jesus knows the heart of a person. All I can say is He looked at me and saw Himself in me and I was accepted into heaven.

Chapter 3

Everything Is Right
"You Did This For Me?!!"

❖

When they first took the breathing tube out of my mouth, I looked up at the person who was sitting by my bed and singing a song about Jesus. A friend of mine I had just met in February of that same year named, Anthony. His job at the hospital was to help with the breathing machines. He and his wife, Monique, had become good friends of ours. So, when I took that first big breath it was like coming out of water. I knew I had died, and I looked at Anthony and said, "You know, Anthony! You know I have seen Jesus! You need to go tell Monique and your church. You do not have to hope there is a Jesus. He is real. And you know I have seen him!"

All I could hear him say in a deep voice was, ''Yeah.'' I saw a big smile on his face, with maybe a tear or two, every time I repeated myself. "I saw Jesus!" I told him over and over.

Something Must Have Really Gone Wrong!

Later, my family came in. I had up until that time, not really known what happened to me that caused me to die.

So, when I saw my parents come through the curtain in ICU, I said to myself, "Something must have really gone wrong," because I knew that they did not call family in, unless you were dying or had died.

My parents live in a little town called Atwater in California, and I had remembered they were out of town visiting my mother's sister in Texas. I knew they had come a long way to see me. So when they came through those curtains I knew I had been in big trouble. Now when my oldest brother came through those curtains, I knew something had really gone wrong! He also lived in California.

My mother came to the left side of the bed, my dad stopped at the foot and my brother came to the right side of the bed. I looked at my mother and said, "Mom, I have seen Jesus three times, and the first time He said, *No, it is not your time. Go back.*" I was really excited. I said to her, "Jesus said the second time, *No, it is not your time. Go back.*" Then I said to my mother, "Jesus said to me a third time, *NO, IT IS NOT YOUR TIME. GO BACK!*" and I told them I cried. I also had a word for each of them from Jesus. I cannot tell you what He said to them. They are the only ones whom I can tell what Jesus said to them. I told them the story of seeing Him three times, and Him telling me it was not my time and to go back.

Thank You, Thank You, Thank You....

Again, I repeat that I know everything is RIGHT where Jesus is and there is nothing wrong. Some say it is peaceful, but it far exceeds past peace because there is nothing to be peaceful from.

When I first got there before Jesus, all I could do was say, "YOU DID THIS FOR ME?!! THANK YOU, THANK YOU, THANK YOU, THANK YOU, THANK YOU, THANK YOU!" I could have said this for the next 3000 years or more, and still would have wanted to keep going.

Jesus is bright and we that are RIGHT with Him can look at Him. He is brighter than our sun, but we can still look at him. There is nothing wrong everything is RIGHT! When I say everything is RIGHT, I mean, everything is RIGHT! We seem to think of everything being peaceful there with Jesus. And we are right in the sense that we need peace from the pain that is in this world now.

> **John 14:1-6 (NKJV)**
> **"Let not your heart be troubled; you believe in God, believe also in Me. In My Father's house are many mansions; if *it were* not *so,* I would have told you. I go to prepare a place for you. And if I go and prepare a place for you, I will come again and receive you to Myself; that where I am, *there* you may be also. And where I go you know, and the way you know." Thomas said to Him, "Lord, we do not know where You are going, and how can we know the way?" Jesus said to him, "I am the way, the truth, and the life. No one** (the Greek word is "oo-dice" meaning nothing) **comes to the Father except through Me.**

When I first got there, all I wanted to do or could do was praise Jesus. As I said earlier, I could have done it for the next 3000 years or longer and not stop. It seemed to me, at the time, I knew what to do. No one had to tell me. I just knew what to do. I know we praise Jesus and Father God, no one else. The only ones who receive praise are the Father and Jesus in heaven, they are THE ONLY ONES.

Where Was The Holy Spirit?
I need to stop and say right here, that I did not mention the Holy Spirit because His main work is here on earth. It is not that He is not there, for we that know Jesus as Lord and

Savior have been told through the bible that the Holy Spirit will be with us always.

John 16:14 (NKJV)
14 And I (Jesus) **will pray the Father, and He will give you another Helper, that He may abide with you forever**

So I still had the Holy Spirit abiding with me in heaven. He was abiding inside of me. I have said many times to many people - If we only understood who we have within us, those of us who know Jesus as Lord and Savior. We have the fullness of God inside of us. Some day I will have to go into more detail about our relationship with the fullness of God within us.

Praising Him Was All I Needed
Now, back to where I left off. Everything within me praised Him. Everything I was made of cried out in praise to Jesus. Not my body (it stayed here on earth), but my spirit and soul - the real me.

I tell people sometimes, that if I had taken my body and it had 10,000 mouths, they all would have been praising the Father and Jesus. During the praising it seem like I was turning into God's LOVE. I had pure JOY. It seems to me that you live off the praising. You did not need any food. Praising Him seemed to be all you needed. He had met all my needs. I say that because everything was right. Everything was right with me, every living being around me and everything was right with my relationship with God.

However, when you are there with Jesus you are not thinking of what you left here. You are thinking of what He did for you to get there. When I said, "you did this for me, thank you, thank you, and thank you," I was thinking of how He died on the cross for me and because of that action, I was there with Him. Not what I did, but what He did when I accepted Him as my Lord and Savior.

I Saw Jesus On The Cross

I remember looking up to Jesus and seeing Him hanging on the cross for me. He was not at the time hanging on the cross, but for some reason I could see Him hanging on the cross within my thinking of Him. I knew what He did on the cross was for me. I knew that, I knew. The only reason I was there is because of what He had done for me, and I knew it. I knew I was complete or perfect because of what He had done. I knew He saw Himself in me and I was allowed into Heaven. I knew none of my works had gotten me in. It was all of His works. Even the good works I did was Him working through me. And it seemed like heaven was made just for me. I knew it was for others also, but it just seemed as if it had been made for only me.

My Place, My Space

I came to really understand what He intended when He said *"I go to prepare a place for you"* (John 14:2). I knew I was in my place. No one could take my place. He loved me so much that Jesus made a place just for me and no one else could take My Place, My Space.

John 14:2 (NKJV)
In My Father's house are many mansions; (mansions literally means dwellings place, a stopping place or resting-place) **if it were not so, I would have told you. I go to prepare a place for you.**

{Place: Greek: topos, Definition: 1) place, any portion or space marked off, as it were from surrounding space 1a) an inhabited place, as a city, village, district 1b) a place (passage) in a book, 2a) the condition or station held by one in any

31

company or assembly 2b) opportunity, power, occasion for acting. a spot (general in space, but limited by occupancy)}

I Had No Memory Of Sin

Another reason I said "You did this for me," is because it was like I had never sinned in my whole life. I knew I had been set free from true death (sin), and it could not keep me from Jesus and the Father. I had no remembrance of sinning at all. And I knew Jesus could not have reminded me, for I was forgiven and He did not remember any of my sins. Again I knew that I knew, that I knew, and I know.

I did not want to leave. It was not that I did not love my wife, children, other family member or friends. It was because everything was just right as I said before. I knew I could never be separated from my Father and Jesus. I came to understand true death is being separated from God. I came to realize that no one could hurt me.

Chapter 4

Pressing In

❧

Marilyn, my wife, currently works as an Activity Assistant, with the elderly. She has worked in the medical field for the past 34 years in a number of positions: Certified Nurse Aide, Endoscopy Technician, Adult Family Home Manger, Physical Therapy Aide and Home Health Care Aide. At the time of this incident she worked with an organization that contracted her out to work in local hospitals and nursing homes.

She is the one who led the charge of praying me back to life on this earth. I call her the "General of Prayer". What you are about to read is her account of what she went through and how she battled to get me back on this earth. In her story are key points to winning battle against the devil and his army of demons. As you read this chapter, there are 10 biblical keys she used to win this battle. Obviously, she won.

Marilyn's Testimony

Thursday, May 4th - "I discovered that Dean was in the St. Francis Hospital Emergency Room at 12 noon after checking my voice mail. There was a message from one of the nurses telling me I needed to pick Dean up and take him home. I was working at another hospital and told the nurse I needed to leave. "When I got to the hospital, Dean was asleep from the pain medication they had given him. The Emergency Room doctor then told me that Dean had kidney stones and a kidney infection with one of the stones located high up on his right side, which was the one that was causing Dean the most pain. The doctor suggested Dean stay over-night to get IV antibiotics and fluids. Dean was in-and-out of the conversation due to the sedation caused by the pain medication.

"Later that evening, a Urologist (kidney specialist) came in to see Dean. He told us that it would be a good idea to have the stones blasted by ultra sound on Friday morning and Dean would not have to endure all that pain. We agreed, knowing Dean would be home the next day. When I left the hospital, Dean was having chills and a fever, but sleeping in intervals."

Friday Morning, May 5th - "Dean is still out of it, due to the medication and a temperature of 104, but still went into surgery. When we went into the surgery waiting area to answer questions, Dean asked at one point if the process was over when he had not even gone into the operating room.

"After the surgery, Dean was in recovery for almost three hours. I spent the last half hour with him in recovery. While we waited, the doctor who had administered Dean's pain medicine while he was in surgery came and told me Dean had a very bad infection and needed to go to Intense Care Unit (ICU) to receive fluids, more antibiotics, and to be observed. I talked to my husband while in recovery. He was complaining about the oxygen mask being uncomfort-able, and the nurses changed it for him. Dean was attached to different IV pumps in his arm. When we got to the room in ICU, I only talked to my husband briefly when the ICU doctor told us they wanted to put a pic-line in Dean's neck so they could take away some of the lines in his arm, and if so, a pic-line would be easy if they needed to draw blood for tests. Dean understood that this was going to happen as I then left for them to start the procedure.

"The nurse came into the waiting area to get me, but when I got to the room, the pic-line was already in Dean's chest. I looked at my husband and could see he was hardly breathing and his lips looked ashy or gray. I asked what happened and the doctor told me they reached a blockage in Dean's neck. I was told immediately they needed to intubate (put a tube down Dean's throat) or else he could die, and there was no time to think about it.

"At that time we lived 5 minutes from the hospital and I left as they were doing this procedure to pick up some things (of course praying on the way). As I drove onto the street, the surgeon called me on my cell phone to tell me my husband coded (his heart stopped) and they were doing CPR (Cardiopulmonary Resuscitation). All I could say was, "What?"

"I called our son and daughter, Gabriel and Tiffany, who were away at college, to tell them to pray for their dad. I continued home praying more intensely, and calling others asking them to pray also. I called a friend who was on her way to the hospital and she said she would come by to pick me up. "When we got there, we did not see Dean right away for they were still working with him. Of course, I got in touch with Dean's parents. They had been visiting relatives in Texas and had to return to California prior to coming to Washington. They talked with the doctor and came as fast as they could. The doctors worked on Dean for 1 hour and 45 minutes. It was during this time, friends showed up in the waiting area and we prayed together in faith for Dean. After we prayed, I felt compelled to sing a song of praise and glorify the Lord."

Key 1:

She first reached out to those she believed would stop and pray. I needed prayer, she needed prayer, and the doctors needed prayer. Later in this book I will tell you about those prayers. I saw them as I was going to heaven and as I was coming back from heaven.

Key 2:

In the midst of the storm she praised God. She started to press into God and not run away from Him.

"The doctor came and told me how touch-and-go things were, and they would know more by morning. Dean was being prayed for in many places throughout the world. We did not demand God in prayer, we did not beg Him, but we asked the Father in Jesus' name. We thanked the Lord God that Dean was healed by the stripes of Jesus. I refused to doubt, but trusted the Word of God for His promise concerning Dean's life.

"I knew I had access to the throne of grace and that I could go boldly as a child of the Most High. Not only did I ask, but also I thanked the Lord for what He was doing in Dean even though the circumstances looked bad. I purposed in my heart not to blame God, for it is the devil that comes to steal, kill, and destroy. Jesus comes to give abundant life (John 10:10) and I claimed that life for my husband."

John 10:10 (NKJV)
The thief does not come except to steal, and to kill, and to destroy. I (Jesus) **have come that they may have life, and that they may have it more abundantly.**

Key 3:

She had a close walk with God before this incident had happen. She was reading her Bible and praying on a continual basis. She knew what the Bible said about this situation. She knew that Jesus came to give abundant life and Satan came to steal, kill, and destroy. So she went to battle knowing what her God came to do for me. That was to give abundant life and at that time I was not living that life.

"It was all so crazy and so sudden. Before I left the hospital, Dean's body was already filling up with the fluids they were putting in him. I felt the need to go home and battle the enemy, for I did not know what the rest of the night would bring Dean. A friend stayed overnight with her son. Before the night was over, Dean was on several medications, including insulin. "When I arrived home, I cried. I thanked the Lord for what a good husband Dean has been (he put up with me). I thanked the Lord for him being a good father to our children. I released the angels of God to be encamped roundabout Dean. I did not get much sleep that night and found myself on the floor the next morning, as I would do the next three mornings praying in the spirit. I still believe there is power in the shed blood of Jesus and I covered Dean in that blood.

Saturday Morning, May 6th - "Dean's blood sugar was 500 and I was told that he needed to be transferred to a different hospital, Tacoma General, to be on Kidney Dialysis continually, because his kidneys did not function at all during the night and his body was going into septic shock. Dean's body was very large from the fluids. He was on 100% ventilation (the machine was doing the breathing for him). Dean went by ambulance that day with a nurse to care for the pumps, the breathing tube, and to suction him if needed.

"I could see that even through this relocation the Lord caused Dean to be transferred to a hospital they normally would not have sent him to. Later on, I had been talking to the supervisor of the nurses that were in charge that day. I knew her since I had worked at this hospital before. She was very surprised that Dean was my husband and was very glad that she had chosen to take him at Tacoma General Hospital.

"Most of the time a patient coming from St. Francis in Federal Way would go to their bigger local sister hospital, which should have been St. Joseph Hospital in Tacoma. She said when she got the call that day to take this crucially ill patient from St. Francis Hospital she knew she should. So as the nursing supervisor she accepted Dean as a patient and when asked by the charge nurse why she was doing it, she said, "I did not know, but I felt that we should." The Lord is good!

"Dean had a very good nurse on duty that morning at the hospital he had been transferred to. The nurse was very positive and I knew that we would get along just fine. Dean was hooked up to dialysis right away. He just laid there without a clue of what was going on. Many came to pray for him and many made themselves available to me if I needed anything. I refused to accept a negative report. I did not deny there were negative reports, I just refused to accept them, and refused to let those reports be the final answer. One doctor told me it could be a long time before Dean would be back to himself, and there could be a possibility of brain damage. I then told him that it did not have to be a long time."

Key 4:
She heard what the doctor said to her, and did not argue with him about his diagnosis, but she kept her mind on what the Bible said. The doctors were doing the best they could, but Marilyn knew that Jesus could do better. So she stuck with what Jesus said.

"When I got home that night, I prayed for Dean long, hard and loud. I told the devil who comes to steal, kill and destroy to take his hands off my husband. My body felt as if it was on fire as sweat dripped onto my nightshirt. It got so wet I took it off laid it on a chair. I took the shirt with me the next morning to the hospital and laid it on Dean's head."

Acts 19:11-12 (NKJV)
Now God worked unusual miracles by the hands of Paul, so that even handkerchiefs or aprons were brought from his body to the sick, and the diseases left them and the evil spirits went out of them.

Key 5:
She was acting on what she had read Paul had done in the Bible. She knew the power of God was on her that night before and wanted that power transferred to me. She had read in the Bible how God's healing power was transferred through clothes and healed.

"Tiffany and Gabriel were in constant prayer themselves, and had put their dad on a prayer chain with several of their friends in school.

"I did not want anything negative spoken over my husband or to him, nor did I want any negative or hopeless prayers prayed. I remember saying to the Father, "I curse every negative word and prayer spoken over or to my husband in the name of Jesus!" I really did not want anyone going in, feeling sorry for Dean, or to think that there was no hope. Death and life are in the power of the tongue, and I made sure my tongue spoke life, for THE WORD OF GOD IS LIFE! I did not have time to feel sorry for Dean and I made no time to feel sorry for him. I felt I was in a battle and I wanted to win."

Proverbs 18:21 (NKJV)
Death and life are in the power of the tongue, And those who love it will eat its fruit

Key 6:
She protected me from negative people and prayers.

Key 7:
She was in this battle to win and whatever godly sacrifices it took she was going to do.

Sunday, May 7th - "The Word of God was preached to some of us in the waiting area and we sang praises. We were still not giving up on Dean. My daughter phoned me and told me to read Psalms 40. My son was calling everyday to talk to the doctor or nurse about his dad's condition. There was a time when the thought came to my mind, "get the funeral ready." Immediately, I brought my thoughts into captivity to the obedience of Christ and I told the devil he was and is a liar. I continued to thank God for His promise in Psalms 103:3, for forgiving all Dean's iniquities, and healing all of Dean's diseases."

Psalm 103:3 (NKJV)
Who forgives all your iniquities, Who heals all your diseases

"GLORY! Dean did respond this day but does not remember. Dean opened his eyes and looked around as to say, what is going on? I told him I loved him as also one of our friends who was with me. The nurse did not want him to get too excited, and so increased the sedative and put him back to sleep."

Key 8:

She kept her mind on the Word of God, even when it was not looking good for me. She took control of her thinking and kept it on God's promises.

Monday, May 8th - "Dean's parents are here. Praise God! For the next few days my mother-in-law and I sang to Dean, read James 5:13-15, and anointed him with oil."

James 5:13-15 (NKJV)
Is anyone among you suffering? Let him pray. Is anyone cheerful? Let him sing psalms. Is anyone among you sick? Let him call for the elders of the church, and let them pray over him, anointing him with oil in the name of the Lord. And the prayer of faith will save the sick, and the Lord will raise him up. And if he has committed sins, he will be forgiven.

"Sometimes Dean's father would go somewhere else to say his prayers.

"I was tired in the body, but my spirit was strong. I was so tired one night, when I arrived at the house, I turned the car off, put my head back and fell fast asleep. When I awoke, I went into the house and prayed. All this happened so fast and unexpectedly. How could something so minor turn out to be so major, so suddenly? I continued to press in closer to the Lord."

Key 9:

She kept pressing into God and relying on God's strength.

"During the past days the doctors would see Dean improve and then slip back to where he had been before. One day he would have a temperature, and they would take him to get a CAT scan to see if the infection had spread. Then the test would come back negative. His white blood count would go up and the potassium would be low. One day he would be down 50% on the ventilator, and that evening it might go back up. I was still trusting God. Dean was on six different medications and most was for his blood pressure, of which one of the medicines was detrimental to Dean's health, I was told by the doctors.

"One of our friends prayed for Dean with such compassion that he kissed Dean's feet as he was praying, he had no idea of the condition my husband's feet were in. Dean's toes were purple and black from the medicine and he had lost feeling in them. We found out later, the doctors were planning on cutting his toes off. Dean also had a feeding tube in for a couple of days toward the end of his stay in ICU."

Tuesday, May 9th - "Dean's healing was taking place fast. It surprised the doctors and nurses and other staff who knew of his case. One doctor would say, he is getting better but we still need to take it slow. Another doctor would say, "Wow he's improved 200-300% in such a short time."

"Many things still happened as Dean's body was healing. The nurse was extremely happy when Dean could follow commands and told the doctor the next day that he was still following commands and that Dean had not skipped a beat. The night of May 9th, I came home and purposed in my heart that I would spend all night in prayer for Dean and found out the next day that a friend said he was tired of the situation and that he would be in prayer all night."

Wednesday Morning May 10th - "Five young boys from High School showed up to pray for Dean during school hours. These boys touched the heart of the nurse that morning and he said he would never forget the prayer and love, and the presence he felt in the room.

"This day he was also taken off the ventilator and dialysis. The nurses asked Dean if he was in any pain, and he shook his head no. They also explained the procedure for removing the breathing tube, and that another breathing treatment would have to be given a half hour later to make sure he could stay off the ventilator.

"The nurses told my in-laws and I to take a long lunch break. Prior to leaving for lunch I spoke in Dean's ear and said to him, "Breathe for me, breathe for your children and breathe for your friends, BREATHE!" He shook his head yes. Dean had a puzzled look on his face, as to say, "What happened?" Dean had this look before but was unable to speak because of the tube. By this time, Dean was down to taking 1-2 medications. "Praise God! Psalms 68:35 was one of the scriptures I held on to, for I needed God's strength and His power."

Psalm 68:35 (NKJV)
O God, You are more awesome than Your holy places. The God of Israel is He who gives strength and power to His people. Blessed be God!

Key 10:
She knew whose power and strength was helping her through.

"Upon returning to the hospital after a great lunch with one of our friends, it was awesome to see Dean sitting up in bed. It was good to hear his voice again. It was a great celebration. Many of the nurses who did not have Dean as a patient came to celebrate his recovery. The nurses were glad to see someone who had made it through all of this, also because it was Nurse's Week and they needed to have a happy ending themselves. "Other staff came as well to see the progress Dean had made, the only word used was,

"Miracle," and boy did we know that! Some came even a couple of days later and they were calling him the "Miracle Man." The fluid was leaving Dean's body and his kidneys were working fine.

"Then Dean asked the big question, "Would you please sit down and tell me what happened to me?" When I told him, he cried and of course, I told him more than once. He wanted to know every detail. It really touched him to know so many cared and prayed; many that we had never met before and some we have yet to meet. Dean was able to get up for about 15 minutes in a chair. This was the first night I stayed with him. I was his nurse that night."

May 14th, Mother's Day - "Dean was moved to another floor. He walked down the long hall to the family visiting room. Dean could not feel his toes, for they were numb. The doctors were still in awe of the miracle that had taken place before their eyes. Dean spent 13 days in the hospital, and 9 of those days were in ICU.

"The effective, fervent (red-hot) *prayer of a righteous man avails much* (James 5:16). We do give God Almighty all the glory for He is faithful to His Word."

May 16th - "Dean came home, where he stayed for one and a half months. When Dean returned to work, he worked half days for 5 weeks. Dean's toes are completely healed. He is not taking any medications. After the 5 weeks, he was back working full time. Dean has had several check-ups and tests since he has been home and the doctors had given him a clean bill of health. One doctor told Dean he should tell the story of the miracle that he is alive. Another doctor told Dean, "A lot of people prayed hard for you." Another doctor said, "I was so scared, I have not been that scared in a long time because things happened so fast."

"Dean has been back to the hospital to visit and they are still saying what a miracle it is. They had him come one day to make rounds, so that others on staff could see him.

"Later we found out that when the doctor blasted the stones, the poisons from the infection got into his bloodstream and all of his vital organs had shut down. One nurse told us later that we have bad outcomes with these cases.

"Psalm 14:1 says, *The fool has said in his heart, "There is no God."* Well, there is a God, He is alive, and miracles do happen. He is the Great Jehovah, God Almighty, Lord of Lords and King of Kings! I bless the readers of this testimony in Jesus name. My prayer for you is that you would take up your cross and follow Jesus daily, and that you would walk a life pleasing to Him. That He would become the lover of your soul as He is mine, in Jesus' name." - **Marilyn Braxton**

Chapter 5

I Have Seen Jesus

✣

As I said earlier, I knew I had died and looked at Anthony, who was one of the people who was helping to remove the breathing tube from my throat, and said, "You know Anthony, you know I have seen Jesus. You need to go tell Monique and your church. You do not have to hope there is a Jesus, you do not have to wish there is a Jesus, He is real. And you know I have seen him!"

Anthony was a friend of Marilyn and mine. We had met him and his wife four months earlier at a bed and breakfast in a small town in Washington. He and his wife pastor a church in Tacoma, Washington. He also worked at the hospital I was at, on life support machines. He was assigned that day to help take me off the machine that was helping me breathe.

I just remember telling him that I had seen Jesus and to go tell everyone he knew. As I told him he just looked at me with a big smile and say, "Yeah, yeah, yeah," with tears coming down his cheeks.

Jesus Is Bright

What did Jesus look like? Jesus is bright. What color is He? Bright. He was not a real color at all as we know here on earth. He was brighter than our sun on a hot sunny noonday and yet you can look at Him. It seemed to me if you were not RIGHT with Him, you would be burned up by this brightness. But those who were RIGHT with Him, could look at Him and have perfect joy. But I knew that if you were not RIGHT with Him, then terror was what you would experience. You had to look at Him with a pure heart. Again, I say it was more than peace, because there just isn't anything to be peaceful from.

His Feet

I saw his feet. They are just like John from the Bible said in Revelations 1:15. The feet did look like metal, gold, silver, tin and many more colors of metals, but the light around them really gave off the shine of fine brass. I knew this was the glory of Jesus. He still has the wounds from where the nails pierced his feet. But what really got me, was the love His feet showed me. He loved me so much that I did not have to look at His face to experience the love He has for me. I did not have to see another part of Jesus to know how much He loved me. His feet expressed His love for me. If all I saw was His feet, I knew He loved me. It was not only that He loved me, but it was like I was the only one He loved in all of His creation. I knew He loved others but it seemed as if I was the only one. I like to tell others, His feet loved me.

His Hands

From that point, I looked at His hands and experienced the same love. Yes, you can see the nail piercings that took place in His hands. But again, it was the love that was coming out of them to me that expressed His love for me. If I was to only have seen His hands and not another part of Him I would have known how much He loves me. I sometimes, in telling this part of the story to others, will put my hand in their face telling them if all you saw was His hand, His hand would say, *"I love you and only you."* You would know He loves others, but it would still seem as if he only loved you. Some have just smiled; others have cried, and others could only say, "WOW!"

His Body

Just like the Bible says in 1John 4:7, *God is love.* As I looked at other parts of His body, I experienced over and over again, the love of Jesus just for me, coming from all those different body parts. His body could only express His love for me.

I saw what His body went through just for me. I saw what it cost for me to be there, and have a relationship with God Almighty. I did not know before this happened, how much it cost in pain to his physical body, for us to have a relationship with God. But, He still bares the scars of what He suffered for us. This is best described in the book of Isaiah.

Isaiah 52:14-15 (NKJV)
Just as many were astonished at you, (Jesus) So His visage was marred more than any man, And His form more than the sons of men; So shall He sprinkle many nations. Kings shall shut their mouths at Him; For what had not been told them they shall see, And what they had not heard they shall consider.

His body showed me why we have the right to have a relationship with God. Why we that know Jesus as Lord and Savior, have the right to live forever with God. Why we have the right to be in heaven and not in hell. Now, don't take this wrong. Jesus is more beautiful, wonderful, and glorious than I can explain. You stop looking at Him with eyes, but from the heart. You get to see Him as He is, but it is from your heart. I came to understand that He advocates for us with His whole being.

1 John 2:1 (NKJV)
My little children, these things I write to you, so that you may not sin. And if anyone sins, we have an Advocate with the Father, Jesus Christ the righteous.

His Face

I was on my hands and knees and I looked into His face. How do I tell you what His face looks like? His face was as if it were liquid crystal glass made up of pure love, light, and life. I am not saying His face is that, but what it looked like to me. His face seemed to change as I looked at Him. His face seemed to change shapes a number of times as I looked at Him. Jesus did have a face just like most humans, but it was changing into different human-like faces. Not big changes, but every time I looked at Him it seemed to change.

I know inside of me, that this change was very important. I just at this time do not have the words to tell what it really means. His face had the colors of the rainbow and colors I cannot describe inside it. All these colors appeared at the same time in His face. It has been hard to explain heaven in English. I know how John and others felt trying to put this in human words.

It was His face changing and all the colors in His face. They were changing all the time and they were bright. They were also part of Jesus and yet they would leave His being, and the colors were alive. They came out and off Him as the waves of the ocean coming on to the shore. I was seeing the colors and I was part of the colors. I was in the colors, and the colors were coming out of me. I was seeing Jesus, and I was a part of Jesus. I was in Jesus, and Jesus was shining out of me. I would see the brightness. The brightness was around me. I was part of the brightness, and brightness was shining out of me. All of it was life. So what color is Jesus? He is bright. He is not a color as we know colors.

Also, many of the glorified beings there did not look human. I will cover this later in the book. At the time I was looking at His face, I did not look at any other part of Him. I just wanted to praise Him. I knew that is what you did when you see Him. I wanted to praise Him forever.

His Head

On His head was a crown that looked like the sun in all its glory. This crown was really bright, with rays going up and out in the atmosphere of heaven. I could not see any end to the rays. Now to me, I knew the rays had something to do with healing. I have not found the words or understanding to be able to say how, but they do. The rays intertwine with His hair. His hair was like John said in Revelations.

Revelation 1:14 (NKJV)
His head and hair were white like wool, as white as snow

Now, to me it looked more than white and tube-like. The hair like tubes, wrap around the rays. As I looked at His hair and crown, I again experienced His love for me.

He Is Love

Everything about Him is love. Yes, love for you; and it seemed as if the love is only for you. Yet you know in yourself that he loves all, but the love for you is so personal it seems as if it is only for you. You know He has cared for you forever and will care for you forever. You did not want to leave this kind of outpouring of love for you. When you looked at any part of His body, you knew He loves you so much. His love is alive. It is more than just a sense.

His brightness is before you, around you, part of you and in you. And one more thing - you are becoming His love. Yes, you are His love. Jesus truly loves us.

Chapter 6

My God Is

❧

B efore you read my daughter's account of what she experienced when I died, here is a little background on Tiffany A. Wright (Braxton). She was attending college at Northwestern University near Chicago, Illinois. She was in her third year there when this happened to me. She graduated with a degree for teaching in 2007. She has been walking with Jesus for a number of years now, and has led a many people to Jesus while attending college. Our Father God has blessed her in a number of ways over the years and this is just one. As you read, you can see her first love is God. Read and enjoy. Grow in the knowledge of our Lord Jesus.

Tiffany's Testimony

"I have to say that my experience with the attack and later recovery of my dad was a hugely, significant time in my relationship with God. I admit that there were times when I thought that I might lose my father. I thought of how he might never see me get married and that my kids could grow up without his spiritual guidance as an amazing grandfather. This was deeply testing.

"When I found out that my dad was in the hospital, I initially did not think much of it. He was having kidney stone problems and had gone through it before. Even when I found out he was going into surgery, I was not alarmed because I had actually been with him before when they had taken care of kidney stones years before. It was not until I got the call from my mother, "Tiffany, they had to do CPR on your father! Pray!"

"I got this call at a very convenient "God moment." I go to the International House of Prayer in Chicago weekly on Friday nights. The previous week, a man came and spoke about whether we truly believe that God is the Living God. I went through the week saying to myself "God, you are the Living God." This truth was starting to stick, and I had decided that I would take care of any doubt issues I had of God living, being good, and being faithful. I got the call after having done so.

"I called my boyfriend, Jason, (now husband) immediately. He said he would be praying and assured me not of God's goodness, but of God. Thankfully, my good friend Jen was with me for support also. She has always been that light that no matter how closed you are you know you can trust her. So I told her and she was nothing but smiles as she prayed in faith with me for my father, and felt God telling her it was going to come out good.

"I prayed the rest of the way home, and all that night I was in and out of sleep. When I woke up, I knew I had to get out of my dorm, so I could really pray. Thankfully, my friend Cory, who had also been with us the previous night, was going to the House of Prayer during the day. I gladly went.

"When I got to the House of Prayer, I sat for a while, getting rid of any doubt and questions that I had. My boyfriend called me and told me he had been out in the woods praying for my family and my dad all day. He once again made sure that I did not doubt that my father would live. Jason was so important in making sure that I dealt with any doubts that came up and that I did not even play with them in my head.

"I also had the opportunity to pray for my father over the phone. My mom put the phone up to his ear and I prayed over him. This was one of the most difficult moments in my life, and at a time when I was glad that I was not there with him. In between the tears, I was able to pray a prayer of faith over him.

"When I went back into the prayer house, I prayed for his healing even more so, and was reminded of the passage when David loses his son. David fasts and prays for his baby boy, until the baby dies. Right after he dies, it says that David goes to the temple to worship the Lord. In remembering this passage of the Bible and David's reliance on God no matter what the situation was, and how David still recognized God's goodness, I really checked my heart for any wrongs within.

"First, was making sure that no matter what, I would continue to pray for the sick even if my dad had died. This was because I needed to go at this with a pure heart that served God alone, not any results.

"Second, was making sure that I would not come out blaming God if he did die. That I would not think God was a bad God, or unfaithful.

"These were two main things to deal with before I prayed, because I wanted to pray with a pure heart, and an undivided heart. I did not believe my dad would die, but I needed to make sure that I was not praying with selfishness, but of wanting God's will.

"So, I then began to pray, most of it being simple worship. I wrote the following about God as I focused on his goodness:

My God is faithful
My God is holy
My God is wonderful

My God is mighty
My God is magnificent
My God is glorious
My God is powerful
My God is victorious
My God is God
My God reigns
My God is love" - **Tiffany A. Wright**

On March 29, 2008, I walked my daughter down the aisle to marry Jason Gomillion Wright. I could not have picked a better man to marry my daughter. I must say it was a great day for me to be there, to see Tiffany get married. I am greatly looking forward to being a wonderful grandfather to their children.

Chapter 7

What Did I See In Heaven?

❦

When I died, I knew where to go. There was no one telling me where to go. I was like a salmon going home. No one had to tell me. When I got there, I knew I was supposed to be there. I was in my place. And everything was RIGHT. I was right where I was supposed to be. I was home. I was home. I WAS HOME!

What is that home like? Not like here. First, everything is alive. Everything is alive and there is nothing dead there. I understood true death was not having the Father God or Jesus or the Holy Spirit in your life. Really, just not having God as your Lord and Savior, that is true death.

Back From The Dead? - On The Contrary

I thought that when you died here that is the death the Bible is talking about. But, when you are there, you know death is not being in relationship with God. When I first got there, I knew that because of what Jesus did, I was with the Father and Jesus, and I knew I was truly alive. Everyone here always says I came back from the dead. On the other hand, even some for fun would say, dead man walking.

No...I was alive with the Father and Son. Just like Jesus said in Matthew.

Matthew 22:32 (NKJV)
"I am the God of Abraham, the God of Isaac, and the God of Jacob"? God is not the God of the dead, but of the living."

God has not stopped creating life. I thought it was done with when man and woman were created, not so. Everything where Jesus and the Father are is alive. He does not live in or with death. Our God is pure life, light, and love. And you become what He is - life, light, and love. Life is everywhere in heaven and life is everything in heaven, life is heaven itself. We here, live with death and think there is an end to everything, but there in heaven life goes on and on.

As I said earlier, everything in heaven is alive. The light-like buildings (they looked like light but were not light), the landscape, and atmosphere, I mean everything. The buildings look almost like glass, but they are alive and not glass. They shine with the glory of the Lord. They also can move around from place to place. The buildings are in cities across heaven. What we would call landscape was alive - the trees, flowers, bushes, grass, mountains, hills, valleys, lakes, rivers, and much more that I do not have words for.

Heaven Is Huge
Because of coming from earth and living with death, a thought went through my thinking, "Aren't we going to run out of room, because there is no death and everything keeps on living?" This thought was in and out. It did not have to be answered because it needed not to be asked. There is more room than we think in heaven. There is room for all God has created and will create.

Heaven is big, large, huge, extensive, spacious and expanding. Our universe is like a fragment of protons or neutrons compared to heaven. In other words, this universe is very, very, very small compared to heaven. I came to understand that heaven is expanding, becoming larger as you read this book. There seemed to be no end, and after a moment I did not care if there was. I was with Jesus. How big heaven was did not matter to me, what mattered was that I was with Jesus. That was all that counted. All I can tell people is that where God is, IS BIG!

Distance And Time

Even though there is more space there than here on earth, there is no distance, as we know it here on earth. I seemed to be far from things and yet near. I seemed to be close to the Father's throne and yet far away. If I wanted to be somewhere else in heaven I just had to think it and I was there. For instance, if I had that ability here on earth and wanted to be around the world in China from Seattle, Washington in the United States, all I would have to do is think it, and I would be there. And, I could be back in Seattle by just thinking it.

How long did I stay there? In the hospital transcripts, they have me down and out, or what they call a Prolonged Cardiac Arrest, for 1 hour and 45 minutes. To me it seemed as if I was there a long time and yet a very short time. I had experienced eternity. Even now, life here seems very short. I know I will outlast every problem that comes my way and someday soon, I will be with Jesus.

I hope you, that are reading this now, can come to that understanding. If you know Jesus as Lord and Savior you will outlive every problem you are facing right now and you will outlive every problem you will ever face on this earth. That is Good News!

I came to understand that whether it is 50 years or 500 years, it will be short compared to eternity. How do you put time on eternity? Why would you put time on eternity? Why do we put time on earth? Because we are counting down to the end of time here on earth. There is no end of time there. Everything that had action was a monument. Jesus said He is the *"Beginning and End."*

Revelation 1:8 (NKJV)
I am the Alpha and the Omega, the Beginning and the End, says the Lord, "who is and who was and who is to come, the Almighty."
The Father said He is *"I AM"* in Exodus.

Exodus 3:14 (NKJV)
And God said to Moses, "I AM WHO I AM."

The Holy Spirit is everywhere all at the same time, past, present, and future as Genesis 1:1-2 and John 14:16 states.

Genesis 1:1-2 (NKJV)
In the beginning God created the heavens and the earth. The earth was without form, and void; and darkness was on the face of the deep. And the Spirit of God was hovering over the face of the waters.

John 14:16 (NKJV)
And I will pray the Father, and He will give you another Helper (Holy Spirit), **that He may abide with you forever**

So how and why would we have a measurement of time there? It really is everlasting eternity.

Because there is no time in heaven, there is no age or aging in heaven. Everything is new every moment. That is hard for us to grasp here on earth, but the fact is, there is just no time in heaven. You are outside of time there. Everything is now.

The Atmosphere In Heaven

Now, I will try to describe the most beautiful atmosphere that has been created. I hear people always talking about the atmosphere here, and how great the sunrise or sunset looks. And the most wonderful or gorgeous sky you can ever see here on earth cannot even come close to the atmosphere in heaven. I start out by saying it is bright because of the glory of our God. Jesus and the Father light up everything; there is no darkness in heaven.

I remember my wife driving me home from the hospital and looking out of the car window. Now, that day was a bright May day here in the beautiful Northwest. Since it rains a lot here in Washington State, when you get a clear day it is so beautiful. Everything is green, the water is so blue, the sky also is very blue, and you can see Mount Rainier, to the east which is over 14,000 feet high and the Cascade Mountain range. To the west, you can see the Olympic Mountains. Again, this was one of those days in the Seattle area. And I was looking out the car window with a frown on my face. My wife looked at me and asked me what was wrong. All I could say was, "It is so dull here." In my heart, I was thinking how dull this whole world is compared to heaven. I sometimes try very hard to make this place seem beautiful, in my mind. I know it is to many people, but because of the atmosphere of heaven, I cannot make it happen for me.

Like I said earlier, Jesus and the Father light up everything. Their glory or light shines out of everything. Darkness cannot hide anywhere in heaven.

The atmosphere is something you can experience and not just see. It is a golden, yellow, white. An artist that I know says it sounds like sunrise colors. The atmosphere there reminded me of the rising of the sun on a clear morning here on earth. The atmosphere had the rainbow colors and more colors moving throughout it. The atmosphere looked like curtains moving on a windy day. It looked like a waterfall in reverse. It would be like you looking at one of the great waterfalls on this earth and seeing the water going up the fall, not down. The curtains look like the Aurora Borealis Lights, also known as the Northern Polar Lights in the north polar zone or the Aurora Australis, also know as the Southern Lights in the south polar zone. But again, the atmosphere was a golden, yellow, with the atmosphere alive. I first came to really see how alive it was when it bowed when Jesus said to me the last time, *"No, It is not your time. Go back."* It just folded over and bowed.

The Colors In Heaven

Colors there are bright. I used to say the dullest color there is brighter than the brightest color here. But, there are no dull colors there. There are colors there we cannot see here. More colors then you can think of. Jesus and the Father give off living colors, and they are beautiful, so beautiful. Everything has a color or colors to it. When I saw Jesus, He is bright and the Father is bright, along with the beings that shine. The best way to describe the colors I saw there is like colors of the rainbow. But saying that really does not do the colors justice. There are more of them than any rainbow we see. More colors than I could imagine.

The colors of flowers here on earth, are the closest to the colors I experienced in heaven and yet they have lost their glory compared to the colors in heaven. Flowers have original colors to them. God is not mixing one color to make another color there. They are the color they are. Red is red, purple is purple, green is green and so on and so on. Every color there is the color, no mixing another color to make an original color. You that are going there, get ready to see some colors that will put you in awe, compared to what you see here on earth. The colors on earth don't even come close to what they do in heaven. Colors are alive there, along with everything else.

Jesus' Words Are Alive

I have said before, that Jesus spoke to me with His voice. His voice is Love. His voice is mighty. His voice left Him with power and authority, but when it got to me, it was life, and comfort. Yes, life for me! It was alive when it entered into me, and as I said before, I knew that I had to go back to the earth. Now, the rest of the moments He spoke to me were just from His heart, just like everything else there.

Communication In Heaven

I felt that speaking words there were a waste of energy, or just not important. I have said this to others and they have defended speaking words here on earth. Words being spoken here are important to us. I understand that, but in heaven, Jesus and the Father thought something and it was transferred to me. The other beings thought it and it was transferred to me.

You lack nothing. You do not have any shortcomings. You are perfect, as your Creator is perfect. That is the way it is with all of God's creation there. Because everything is alive they could all communicate with you. All of life there thought it, and it was transferred to me. It was faster and more clear, because you experience it when you communicate with each other.

Everything was RIGHT, so there was no miscommunication with each other. There were no misunderstandings with each other. There was nothing you would have to hide from each other. We all had pure thoughts and every thought was pure. There was a rule that you did not go into any of heavenly creation's thoughts without them giving you permission to. The last being (Satan) that did that is no longer there in heaven. What power we could all have if we just really understood what thinking could do.

Everyone And Everything Praised The Lord

The only time I saw beings open their mouths were when they were singing praises to the Father at the throne.

Every living being and creature praises the Father and Jesus. Every part of God's creation praises God all the time, and no one else receives praise, but only God. There is a part of being there, that you knew that is what you do. It is like breathing air here on earth. I seemed to live off the praise. You lived because of God himself and nothing else.

To hear the flowers praise the Lord is wonderful. The birds sing praise to the Lord. Water praised the Lord. Mountains praised the Lord. Praise came from the atmosphere. Praise was in the atmosphere. Praise was the atmosphere. We all praised Him repeatedly, over and over again. You never seem to run out of things to praise Him for. I can remember thanking Him over and over for being there and loving me so much. I thanked Him for loving everyone here on earth. I thanked Him for making me. I thanked Him; I could go on and on.

Just writing this down reminds me of the fact, that praise did not leave my thinking when I was there. I still praise Him all the time. It is hard for me to stop and to think of other things. It is hard - because of the praising of Him - for me to see what everyone else thinks is so important here on earth. You that know Jesus as Lord and Savior, will experience what I am writing about here. I am sorry I cannot explain it any better than I have.

When I first came out of the hospital and was at home, I would wake up early to see the day awake. That is what I called it. Really, I just wanted to hear the birds sing and see the sun come up. The birds in heaven always praise the Lord with their songs. The birds here on earth do the same, most of the time. And when the sun comes up, it seems to me to be saying, "Praise the Lord." So, I wanted to see this take place every morning, and say along with this creation of God, "Praise the Lord." Every living being and creature praises the Father and Jesus.

Our Connection In Heaven

One of the most fascinating things I experienced, was being connected to everything there at the same moment. Because of this, I came to understanding life in heaven fast. It is like the electricity that connects power to run anything that needs electric energy here. It is like our computer system that is connected to the Internet, which connects us to every computer in the world. God connects every one of His creations together. This gave me great understanding of what I say.

Relating My Experience To You

There is no substance on earth that can come close to what substance God used to create everything in heaven. There is no sin to corrupt what God has made. His creations there are in their purest form. There is no sin to destroy what God has made. So, all I can tell you, and describe, is what something is like. If you have what some call, "an out of body experience" and after the experience, you are not connected to everything, then you can only relate to what you saw from an earthly point of view.

I have come to believe that only those who have truly died can tell you what they saw from a heavenly point of view. The reason is because their body became disconnected from the real them, their spirit. Their bodies stayed here on earth.

When I was there, I did not want to come back, and I was planning on staying. So, I understand what John (who wrote Revelations), Ezekiel, Daniel and David (who wrote most of the Psalms) went through trying to tell others about heaven in earthly terms. As you read on, and if you read the writings of these men in the Bible you will see they use the word "like" a lot, to try to tell us what they saw. I have already used a lot of examples in this book to help you see what I saw, or hear what I heard. But understand, as much as I try to get what I say across to others, I am still coming up way short of what it is really like there. This connection to everything there and everything connected to me just helps me explain it to others better.

One of the best ways I have found for people to connect with what I experienced in heaven, is through the Bible. I have found approximately 90% of what I explain about heaven, somewhere in the Bible. I have met with my Pastor and Assistant Pastor for almost two years now, going over what I experienced in heaven. We have worked together to find verses in the Bible that relates to a specific event that I experienced in heaven. I knew from what Jesus downloaded inside of me that I would find everything I saw in heaven in the Bible. He is not hiding heaven from us. We have just built a number of boxes around our thinking.

Some have said that God did not put everything in the Bible, and I say that most likely is true. But I say to them, until you can tell me everything in the Bible you cannot stand on that statement. I have found so much in the Bible of what I experienced in heaven. Finding the right earthly words is the hard part.

Chapter 8

God Of Miracles

M y son, Gabriel A. Braxton, was 19 years old and was attending Christ For The Nations Bible College in Dallas, Texas. Within his portion of this story, he had a host of friends around his age that loved the Lord Jesus. Many of these young men and ladies, he led to the Lord. A number of his friends prayed and helped him through this trying time. A few of them even came to the hospital to pray for me when Gabriel was still in Texas.

His account of the story is taken out of his journal. As you read on you will feel the love my son had for me as he was faced with his father's death.

Gabriel's Testimony

May 11th, 2006 - "This last week has been crazy! I did not journal for the past seven days because of some events that happened. What I did not mention, is what happened on May 4th, that had to do with my dad. He went into the hospital (St. Francis) because of a kidney stone. I did not think of it as a big deal but my mom called, and asked for me to pray, so, I did.

"I found out my dad had kidney stones and an infection and they were pumping him with antibiotics to get the infection out of his system. It was a miracle that he drove and walked into the hospital by himself. Kidney stones cause serious pain.

"The next day, May 5th, I found out that my dad had to go in for surgery. They were going to blast the stones to pieces and they did. After the surgery, my dad was doing fine. That day Tomo, Luke, Joe and I went to the Rangers game. It was pretty fun. I read my Bible some, and bounced my eyes from some chicken nuggets! They were everywhere. It was crazy. Throughout that day, I had been praying for my dad and some of my friends had been praying for him as well.

"I called my mom a lot because I wanted to know how he was doing. During the Rangers game, I got a call from my mom. It was an urgent serious call. She told me that the doctors were doing CPR on my dad. His heart had stopped. That changed the course of the night but, I guess that is kind of obvious right? I mean, common sense.

"So, Tomo, Luke, Joe, and I prayed and afterwards I walked out to the food area. I began to pray and prophecy over my dad saying that he would live and not die. I bound the devil and commanded my dad's body to work properly. It was intense! I called people and told them to pray but at first, I could not get a hold of anyone.

"Staring at Six Flags from the balcony of the stadium in Dallas, Texas, I started to hate the fact that I was so many miles away from my dad. Joe walked out. I forget what he said but, we pretty much left. I did not stop praying. I kept going at it because I was determined and bent on Gods will to heal my dad. On the ride back in the car, I called my mom and Francine answered the phone. After an hour and a half, my dad was finally stable. What a relief, well, a little relief. Joe thanked God for answering his prayer for performing a miracle.

"I had lost my huge appetite and I just wanted to go home and pray. We got back to the G (guys' tower at college) and I went upstairs. I met up with Sam and he and I went at it in his room. We prayed it up. Later he told me he really did not think it would make sense for my dad to die. During the prayer time, he said to God, It does not make sense to me why Gabe and his sister would have to grow up without a father. "After a while, he went out with his girlfriend at the time and said that I could stay in the room and pray. Of course, I did this, and also prophesied, prayed, commanded and pleaded. I put all I learned about healing into practice and I refused to back down. Curfew was 1 o'clock that night so I planned to pray until at least 12:30 AM.

"During the prayer time, I called my mom to see how my dad was doing. She said that he was urinating which was good because that meant that his kidneys were functioning properly. Around 12:15 AM, I went to Joe, Luke, and Michael's room to see if Luke would take me somewhere to get something to eat. I did not have much of an appetite but I knew I should have something to eat. They were all asleep so Luke did not really want to get up and drive me somewhere at the time. I called Joe's girlfriend who is now his wife, Abbie, and I asked if she could take me somewhere. She said she would. Her roommate, Rhema, prayed with her father about my dad. Rhema said both her and her dad felt a strong anointing. Her father had a huge burden for my dad and the next day they would have the Church pray for him. What a blessing!

"While I was waiting downstairs in the bottom of the G, Luke called my phone and asked where I was. He changed his mind about taking me but Abbie and Rhema were already on their way. Luke decided to go with us too. Joe really had God's favor shine upon him. Abbie is an amazing person. She is so loving and caring. It's amazing. She takes care of Luke and I. It's really sweet of her. So she drove us to Sonic and I ordered a chili dog. The drive and talk with my friends really encouraged me. We had a few laughs and that was good.

"When I got back, I called my mom to see how she was doing. She was crying and saying that she missed my dad. She wanted him to come home. I encouraged her though it was sad and after that, I could not eat. I had a few bites of the chili dog and put it in the fridge. I drifted off to sleep.

"The next day, May 6th, I decided I would spend the day in the prayer room. I was just going to grab my phone charger, my laptop, my pillow, and camp out. Joe went with Abbie to her house to meet her parents. Luke was just hanging around and well, Tomo, who knows what Tomo did that day.

"I remember before I went to the prayer room I was in my room and my mom called. She told me that they wanted to transfer my dad to Tacoma General to have him undergo dialysis because his kidneys were not functioning too well anymore. It was our choice to decide. This was hard because we have had some bad experiences with hospitals in the past. She told me to call my sister, Tiffany, and ask her to basically, give her vote.

"After I got off the phone, I began to cry. I did not know what to do. I told God, I am only 19. I told Him that I didn't know anything about medical stuff. I didn't even want to have a say in it. Then, I called Tiffany. My sister told me to tell my mom to pray about it and decide. I called my mom back and she had the nurse tell me what she was going to do. Personally, I was going to say no but, after the nurse explained that it was not a huge dialysis machine it was easier for me to trust. So my mom said she would do it.

"I cannot recall everything that happened during this time. I do a horrible job of mentioning all the people that prayed for my dad with me and in their spare time. It was something extremely awesome to see and experience. Everyone kept speaking blessings over my dad saying that he would live and that he was going to be alright. I called my mom a lot to see how my dad was doing.

"Later that day, I told my friend Andrew what was going on, and he prayed. Then, he spoke a word over me that I knew was true. He told me to stay strong in faith. I think he even gave me a scripture, but I don't remember. He also told me not to waiver in unbelief and he said, "I do not believe you are doing that." I knew that I wasn't wavering. I knew that the grace of Jesus empowered me to not lose faith, to not lose heart, and to continue in intercession. I called out the prophesies that have been spoken over my dad's life and I said they would continue. "My dad always said our family was a team so I called my mom and sister and prayed with them, claiming that the leader of this team would not be taken away. I started to think about the situation. Then I received a revelation. The devil wanted to take out my dad's kidneys because the kidneys dispose of the toxins in the body and this connected spiritually. My dad has a huge burden to rid sin out of his life, like the kidneys, so the devil was attacking the physical to destroy the spiritual.

"Also, the devil wanted his heart because my dad has a huge heart for people. He loves so much and Satan hates that. So I sent a text message to those who were praying for him and told them what Satan was trying to do. I told them to claim that he would continue to get the sin out of his life, and his heart would continue to grow in love for people. Then, I called my mom and sister and told them. After an intense day of prayer, I was encouraged.

"Luke and I went to get a smoothie and then we chilled in his room with Mike. Danger Dave, well, David, showed up in the room and hung out with us. I have to admit, we talked about girls and Luke's crush. It was good though. I heard that my dad was doing better and I fell asleep in the room. I woke up at 12:59 AM and ran back to room 406 because curfew was at 1:00 AM.

"Sunday morning, May 7th, I got a call from Joe asking if I wanted to go over to Mary Martha's (girls dorm) courtyard and eat some ribs. At first, I didn't want to but after a while I decided I should go and yeah, I forget what happened the rest of the day.

"Monday, May 8th, I had an exam for Life and Teachings of Christ. I didn't really study for it because of all the things that were taking place. I think I did well though. During these days I prayed for my dad a lot and called the hospital a lot to see how he was doing. People prayed with me. When I would call, the nurse gave good reports. Even though the report was good, I still chose to believe God's report. I chose to believe my dad was healed by the stripes of Jesus. That day I went out to eat at Chipotle's with Luke and Joe. It was fun. I learned what to get and how to eat the burrito they made for me. Meaning - I started out using utensils but that was not really working. I should have looked at the directions on the napkin.

"I am not so sure what I did on Tuesday, May 9th. That night I went to Bennigan's with Isaac and Samantha, Toni, Kristina, Anthony, Joel (Anthony's roommate) and Luke. Later that night I learned that my dad was having a rough time in the hospital. My mom told me that my dad was crying some that day. That was one of the things I didn't want to hear. After I heard that, I was so sad. I had to pray.

"I stepped outside and did so. While outside, I called the nurse and she told me that my dad was on 100% oxygen. That was not good because he had just been on 50%. We made it home about 20 minutes before curfew and I asked Wade, one of the Room Assistants (RA) on our floor, if I could go to the prayer room. He said yes and Sam, who as another RA, suggested that I go to the eighth floor prayer room and if it was locked, go to the prayer room on the first floor. So I went up to room 807 and Andrew was in there. He joined me in praying for my dad for about 25 minutes. That was nice of him.

"The next morning, May 10th, I woke up at 5:00 AM to pray for my dad. I couldn't stop praying. That day I had decided to read Proverbs 10. It was the chapter for my dad. I wanted him off the ventilator and that chapter has many promises concerning your mouth. I claimed the blessings of the chapter in my dad's life. I couldn't stop praying that morning. I prayed for him all the way through chapel, which ended at 8:40 AM. "That day, we had an exam for Fred's Evangelism class. I think I did fairly well, though I did not study that much. Wednesday was a big day. It was my last day of college before summer break. "After school that day, Luke, Michael, Joe, and I went out to T.G.I. Friday's to eat. While being there, I saw a kid in a wheel chair that I wanted to pray for. He was gathered around a table with other young kids and some adults taking care of them. I went up to one of the adult ladies and asked if I could pray for him. She said she didn't mind and insisted that I pray for all of them as well. So I prayed for them all. That was a blessing.

"Although things were rough back at home, in the bigger picture, the mission still continued. During that day, my mom called me and told me some extraordinary news. I heard of a miracle that shocked the doctors and had the whole floor rejoicing. They had taken the ventilator out of my dad's mouth. He was doing well. He was speaking, which was cool.

"One of the best things was some news that he gave my mom. He told her that he had died three times, each time seeing Jesus, and Jesus telling him to go back because it was not his time. My dad came out of his sedation with many words to tell people and a lot of information that Jesus had shared with him. How exciting! I told some people and rejoiced myself. After running around helping Joe find some things, we finally settled down to have my last night with them at Applebee's. Joe, Abbie, Luke, and I had a good time.

"The next morning, I would catch my flight back to Seattle, Washington. That night, I slept in Joe, Luke, and Michael's room because earlier that day I had checked out of my room. Joe tried to beat up Luke and me but we survived after hiding in the bathroom for like, seven minutes. Later that night while I was sleeping, Hannah (the daughter of Ron Luce, from Teen Mania) called, and I had the chance to tell her about the awesome testimony. She said it encouraged her. She was having a rough day. That night I went to sleep on the reclining chair in their super messy room. It was really comfortable but I had a bit of a rough night.

"My alarm went off at 5:00 AM. It was May 11th and my flight was going to start boarding at 6:30 AM. Luke and Joe woke up and helped me take my stuff downstairs. I look back on that morning and it's sad, because I miss those guys. My Uncle Larry arrived at 5:30 AM and Luke, Joe, and I said our good-byes.

"I arrived at the airport around 6:00 AM. I had two big suitcases and one of them was super heavy. When I got to the baggage check-in line the first bag went in okay. I figured I would have to pay for the really heavy one. So I threw it up on the scale and it weighed about 70 something pounds. The guy told me I'd have to pay $25 and that was okay with me because I expected that. He was doing a few things and all of a sudden, he told me I could go. So, I didn't have to pay. Jesus reveals Himself to me through things like these.

"The plane ride went well. I sat next to a guy named Ron and he was really nice. Ron and his wife are Southern Baptist and they were on their way to Seattle to catch a cruise to Alaska. When our food came, I asked Ron if he wanted to pray with me for it. I was sitting in the end seat C and he was sitting in the middle seat B with his wife to the left of him in seat A. I leaned over and prayed aloud for the food. The rest of the flight went well. Towards the end of the flight, Ron handed me a card and told me he wanted to take me out to eat next time I am in Texas. That was nice of him. When I arrived in Seattle, Washington, my Uncle Lewis picked me up from the airport. "We drove to my house and dropped my stuff off. My mom was there and it was good to see her. Then, we went to pick up my grandma and grandpa and once we got them, we headed to the hospital. I saw my dad and I got to hug him. It was exciting. Of course, I did not like seeing him in the hospital but I was just glad to see him. I did not like being so far away from him when all those things were going on. He lifted up three fingers and told me he saw Jesus three times. He started to cry when he said this.

"Jon came and visited my dad for about 45 minutes. That was nice of him. After I visited with my dad, my mom took me home so I could shower and then rest. I went back later and stayed the night with my dad. When it was time to sleep though, the nurses and doctors were going to be waking us up periodically throughout the night. My dad told me to hold his hand as we fell asleep listening to Psalms.

"On Friday, May 12th, my dad had to get a pic-line (like an IV line) put in the thick vein right above his heart. I didn't like having to give my input on decisions like this. The doctor went over a list of all the things that could go wrong. My grandma, grandpa, mom, dad, and I prayed about what to do. If we did not have the pic-line put in, the veins in my dad's left arm would have been destroyed because the certain IV medication they recently put in him was not meant to go through small veins. "My grandpa said we should do it. My grandma agreed and I said we should do it. My mom said to go through with it and my dad felt secure about it. Before that, I brought the list over to my mom and said I figured it out. "You see these?" I pointed to the bad side effects. I said, "These are all just fears and God did not give us a spirit of fear." So, God's word gave me a comfort about the situation. When the decision was set, I got anxious to have people leave the room though I didn't show it too much. I did not want my dad to talk. I just wanted them to put the pic-line in and take that other IV out of his arm. Then I went home. "My mom was doing the day shifts and I was doing the night shifts. I prayed the whole way home and called Joe to pray as well. When I got home, I spent the next hour praying for my dad. I know many people do not believe in perfection but I wanted what the doctors were doing to be perfect. My dad had told me to call Pastor Steve and let him know that he was in the hospital and to send him a personal message about friendship as well. I called him and we prayed for my dad.

"After the hour was finished, I called my mom to see what was going on. Inserting the pic-line was successful. Later that night, I went back to the hospital. I put my chair up to the bed and fell asleep next to my dad. I had a good night's rest that night. We had Christian music playing in the background. It was great. Throughout these days, I would help him eat and get him things. It was good for my mom and I to have been there. After a night with my dad, I left Saturday morning.

"It was May 13th. When I got home, I called Lennie and asked him if he wanted to hang out. I asked him to mow the lawn as well and he was nice enough to do so. My dad had been talking about getting the lawn mowed. Lennie and I rode around as we were going to visit my dad. So, we went to visit my dad and while we were there, Pastor Steve and Beth dropped in for a visit as well. They brought my dad a shirt that Josh (Pastor Steve's son) had made for an event he founded called Repossess.

"While Pastor Steve and Beth visited with my dad, Lennie and I left. We went to Arby's and met up with Luke. From there, we went to the Christian bookstore trying to find my mom a Mother's Day gift. I didn't know what to get her. Lennie had a brilliant plan. He told me to get my mom some Ranger Cookies from Marlene's - Perfect! She had not had them in a long time and she would always tell me to get them for her. So, I got a card from the CBS and headed over to Marlene's. As Lennie and I walked up, Marlene's was closing but the lady let us in to grab the cookies. That was nice of her. Afterwards, we all went to eat at Chipotle's. Then, I went back to the hospital. That night was rough for me. I was sick and I felt horrible so I left at 3:00 AM.

"It was Mothers Day, May 14, and I woke up after a rough night. I was hanging out in my parents' room, on the computer. After a while, I left to go be with my dad. Also, earlier that day I had found out that they were moving my dad out of ICU. That was good. So, when I got there, I hung out with my dad in a regular hospital room. They brought me in a cot to sleep on for the night.

"That night I served my dad and helped him out a lot. It was rough. We were up just about every hour, with nurses coming in and out of the room and my dad having nightmares. So we prayed and turned on some Christian music. I think that helped a bit. Around 6:00 AM, my dad woke me up and told me to leave so I could go home and get some rest. I thought it was funny. Here we are being woken up all night and not getting any rest and finally when I fall asleep, he tells me to leave. Ha-ha! That's okay though. There goes my dad, being in the hospital, yet putting others before himself. So I went home and slept.

"So here we are, May 15th – well, sort of. I woke up around 3:00 PM, and immediately had to get up. I didn't do much today. I printed out resumes to get a job this summer. Around 6:10 PM, I started to pray for about 45 minutes. My sister was flying in today. Her flight was going to land at 7:45 PM, and I was going to be the one to pick her up. After praying, I headed to the airport to get my sister. It was good to see my sister. We headed off to the hospital after that.

"When we got to the hospital, my dad was happy to see my sister but he had other visitors inside the room so we waited outside in the waiting room with our grandma and grandpa. The other visitors left and my sister and I had the chance to see our dad. I was coughing a lot so my dad said I could not stay. He wanted me to go home and rest. He said he would be okay. I wanted to stay but I think he said what was best.

"May 16, 2006 - Today was a cool day. My dad came home. That was exciting...and Jesus is amazing!" **- Gabriel Braxton**

Chapter 9

The True Gatekeeper Of Heaven

❧

I came to understand who the real gatekeeper of Heaven is, it is only Jesus. I understood this the last time He told me to *"Go Back."* I saw in His eyes the love for humanity. I saw the love for every girl, boy, woman and man.

I Looked Into Jesus' Eyes

His eyes are like flames of fire with changing colors of red, orange, blue, green, yellow, and many other colors. John said in Revelations 1:14 that, *"His eyes* (are) *like a flame of fire"*. I experienced in His eyes, that they are deep, and full of life. You could get lost in His eyes and never want to come out.

In His eyes I saw the love for every human and creation of God. Again, at first it seemed as if His eyes only had love for me. But, when I thought about someone else, I saw the love for them. It was like He loved only them. So I thought about someone else and the same thing happened. I saw His love for them. I did this with a number of heavenly beings and a few people here on earth.

I saw in His eyes that He wanted everyone there, who are still alive on this earth. He did not want to lose one person or have them go to hell. Jesus wants all people saved. I wish we could understand that. He loves everyone. The Father, Jesus, and Holy Spirit love everyone so much.

During this time, when I looked in His eyes and saw this love, I knew I became that love also. If we have Jesus, we all have that love in us and should be becoming His love for others.

He Loves Us No Matter What

Now, during that time of looking into His eyes, we had this communication in our thoughts, and no words were spoken. I said to Him, "Even child molesters?" As you have read earlier, I had worked with children and teenagers over the past 33 years. During that time, the one issue that came up a lot with the children I had worked with, was sexual abuse by adults. This one issue, to me, seems to do more damage than all the other issues I faced as a counselor. I have seen many people who had recovered from many types of abuse, but every time I had to deal with someone who had been sexually abused, the damage seemed to be the most harmful out of all the other abuses. I would always get upset on the inside of myself.

So as we communicated, Jesus said back to me, *"When you place a person in jail, they get out. They either get out when their time is up, or they get out when they die, but they get out. But when we put a person in hell, they are there for eternity."* Then His eyes looked at me with the fiery red flame and said, *"WHO ARE YOU TO NULIFY WHAT I HAD DONE!"* This came across to me very stern. I also saw His arms outstretched like He was on the cross and He paid the price for_everyone who sinned, or ever will sin, implying that we do not have a right to condemn anyone, since He does not. I knew that I knew - He wanted all people there with Him. He truly wants us there with Him. All people!

Aunt Barbara

I remember seeing one of my relatives in heaven that I had believed would not have made it, my Aunt Barbra.

My Aunt Barbra was my favorite aunt. She lived close to us when I was growing up in California. She would come and take care of us when our parents would go out of town. She was fun to be around, and I could not wait to see her when she came around.

The side that I saw of her when she was on earth did not lead me to believe she was a Christian and would go to heaven, but when I was in heaven, guess who was there? Yes, Aunt Barbra, she must have accepted Jesus as Lord and Savior because that is the only way you get in. Since I did not see her make that relationship with Jesus I had believed in my heart that she did not make it. It is not I who get people into heaven and it is not you that do. It is Jesus.

My wife has led many people to the Lord and their relatives never found out about it. But Jesus does not give up on anyone, even up to their last breath on this earth. It is only Jesus. He is the Gate Keeper.

Chapter 10

Medical Records And Transcripts

❖

B efore this incident took place, I was a very healthy 47 year old male. I had regular physical checkups. Most of these checkups were because I was in the United States Air Force on active duty for 6 years and reserve duty for 14 years. I retired from the reserves with a clean bill of health. The only problem I had after that, was kidney stones in June of 2002, four years prior to this incident.

I went through the same procedure back then for kidney stones as I did for this incident. The biggest difference was staying in the hospital overnight before the operation. In June of 2002 I checked into the hospital that morning and came out in the afternoon of the same day.

The following is taken from the Medical Records we received from both hospitals that I was admitted into. Now, to get these records was not easy, because of the mistakes that were made and the potential of a law suit. The doctor who made the mistakes made it hard for us to receive accurate reports. Finally, we had to get other doctors who worked on my case to give us the information.

It has never been our intention to sue the doctor or the hospital. We just wanted the official medical records to support the medical testimonies we had received from doctors, nurses, and other people who worked in the hospitals.

The other thing about these records is that it has been hard to get a medical professional to read what we have and write it down for this book. We came up against resistance from people not wanting to go on record in translating the medical account. They just did not want to support in writing the number of mistakes that were made by the Urologist and hospital. Again, they did not want to be a part of any potential law suit in the future. So, the following is raw information that will have to be translated by the reader.

During the next 4 years after the first treatment for kidney stones, I did not have any problems with kidney stones or any other illness. I do not remember taking any sick leave for personal illness.

Excerpts Of Information Taken From My Medical Records And Medical Transcripts

Preoperative Diagnosis: Left ureteral calculus and bilateral nephrolithiasis (Kidney stones) and pyelonephritis (urinary tract infection)

Postoperative Diagnosis: Left ureteral calculus and bilateral nephrolithiasis and pyelonephritis

Operation: Cystoscopy with retrograde pyelogram, push back of ureteral calculus and bilateral extracorporeal shock wave lithotripsy

Indications: This delightful 49-year-old gentleman *(really 47-year-old)* presented to the hospital with pyelonephritis and obstruction ureteral calculus. After 24 hours of antibiotic coverage with supplemental antibiotic administration in operation room, he presents at this time for definitive surgical intervention.

Findings: Obstructing calculus in the left ureter is pushed back in the renal pelvis, and a 24-cm 7-french double-J stent is left in place in the ureter and that calculus further targets and both kidneys were fragmented with difficulty.

After 2400 shocks, the procedure was terminated and the patient was awakened and returned to the recovery room in satisfactory condition. There were no complications He tolerated the procedure well. - *This was from a May 6, 2006 report by the surgeon who performed the original operation.*

Excerpts Taken From The Rest Of The Medical Records And Medical Transcripts

- Larger amount of fluid resuscitation for hypertension
- Poorly responsive
- Move legs to pain
- Very cool digits with cyanotic toes
- Acute renal failure
- Secondary to acute tubular necrosis oliguric
- Profound septic shock
- Prolonged Cardiac Arrest
- CPR one hour and 45 minutes
- Septic shock with urasepisis
- Respiratory failure
- Pulmonary infiltrates
- Edema versus adult respiratory distress Syndrome
- Post prolonged CPR
- Post cardiac arrest
- Prolonged resuscitation
- Fulminant sepsis
- Too numerous to count stone in right kidney
- Chest x-rays show the development of diffuse pulmonary edema
- Urine culture sent yesterday is growing greater than 100,000 colonies of E. coli.

- Doctor reports of spent a total of 1 hour and 45 min. total critical care time with the patient not including procedure
- Server sepsis
- Diagnosis of SIRS/Sepsis with hypotension, tachycardia, tachypnea, hypoxemia.
- High risk of disseminated intravascular coagulation.
- Cardiac arrest
- Urasepsis with E.Coli.
- Secondary renal shut down.
- Asystable
- Extubated
- Herodynamically Stable
- Shock liver
- Shock syndrome
- Hemodynamic stress
- On mechanical ventilation
- Paralytic ileus
- Multi-organ failure
- Critically ill
- Prognosis is poor
- Quniton Cathetar and dialysis treatment (risk & Benefits)
- Risk for bleeding complication with ongoing DIC
- Clotting dialysis system given ongoing DIC
- Obstruction urinary stones
- Severely acidotic with a lactic acid as high as 16.
- Poorly responsive
- Requiring High Fi0 Moderate to servers patchy air space
- Opacities in the lungs bilaterally slightly increased. This is ward son for progression of pneumonia.
- Very unfortunate critically ill patient.

After the recovery, I did receive some resistance from the doctor who had performed the operation in taking out a stint that was placed in my body. My wife had to call the doctor and state that she was going to take legal action if we did not receive an appointment to have the stint removed. We did receive an appointment for the next day and the doctor removed the stint.

I asked him at that time what happened to cause my heart to stop. He said that I had a bad infection that he thought was taken care of with some really strong medicine. But for some reason the infection was not affected by the medicine that had been given to me. He said they had not checked prior to the operation if the medicine worked or not, and had assumed it did. It was not until five days later, that they found out from lab reports that the medicine did not have any affect on the infection.

At the time of the incident, the doctor did not know what was going wrong or why my vital organs were shutting down. The doctor told me that if they would not have done everything right I would have been behind the eight ball (dead). If they would have done a process ten minutes earlier or ten minutes later I would have been behind the eight ball.

I did ask him if I had died. He said my heart had stopped, and that every time it looked like it was going to start beating again, it would not. He said they worked on me about 1 hour and 30 minutes (Official record stated 1 hour and 45 minutes). I asked him if he saw this as a miracle and he said it was, and that I should go tell the story.

As you can read, there were a lot of things that just went wrong with the procedures and my body. But God healed it all. Praise God!

Chapter 11

Jesus Wants All People Saved

❖

Everything is right, you are connected with everything and everything is connected with you. What was Jesus doing when I got there? Something I would not have thought of. He was strategizing. He was communicating to these beings in front of Him, which stood in a half circle facing Him. He was strategizing to get more people on this earth to know Him as Lord and Savior.

God is using everything that He can, short of evil, to get people to know Jesus as Lord and Savior. He is looking for people on earth to work with Him in getting people to know who He is. I came to understand how much we are at war. He is urging all of mankind to press into the Kingdom of God. We are so very important to Him! When I was in heaven, I was connected to everything and everyone, and everything and everyone was connected to me. Because of this, I understood just how important we that are on earth are to Him.

Heavenly Interventions

I say that I was surprised, because I believed that after He died on the cross and ascended into heaven, there wouldn't be any need for strategizing - that was it. However, when I look throughout the New Testament there is more than once, times where Jesus is sending angels on what I call "heavenly interventions" to get people saved every day.

We read about some of these heavenly interventions in Acts chapter 8 with the Ethiopian eunuch and Philip; Acts chapter 9 with Saul (Paul) and Ananias; and Acts chapter 10 with Cornelius and Peter. As soon as someone turns to God in his or her heart, He is right there. I tell others there are many people there that we did not think would be there. Also, there are those who we thought would be there, but are not. As it says in Romans chapter 10, God is looking at a person's heart - not just what they say or do.

Everything is right and everyone has the right to be in a place of rightness. Everything there is alive and everyone has a right to live with God forever. I understood, that is why we are here - to tell others of who Jesus is, so that they can go and be with GOD.

The Army Of God

I came to understand there are two units in the army of God. There is a heavenly unit and earthly unit, but they are the same army of God.

The heavenly unit is made up of the angels of God. I saw how the heavenly unit worked. They understood whose government they belong to. They understood whose Kingdom they work for. When Jesus would communicate to them, they showed great AWE (respect). That moment for me, I have not forgotten. One of the other reasons I did not want to leave is because I wanted to be a part of that unit. I wanted to be with His creation that respected Him for who He is - King of Kings and Lord of Lords.

I can remember telling my son later in the hospital room, that I could not sing any songs that did not respect Jesus as King.

I saw how those heavenly creatures would bow before they left Him, and back out as they left. They would not turn their back to Him. They left right and fast on to the assignment He sent them on. I did not see one of them question anything He commanded them to do.

They were sent to fight in the heavenlies. They were fighting evil spirits that belong to Satan's army. I knew that prayer is what moved them. I will cover these two areas, prayer and angels, in later chapters.

Then, there was the earthly unit. The one I was sent back to. The one I did not want to be a part of. I did not want to be a part of this earthly unit because I had already been a part of the heavenly unit. I had seen the complete opposite of what the heavenly unit did. I had done the complete opposite of what the heavenly unit does.

When Jesus told me to *"Go Back"*, on the inside of me, I knew he was saying, *"I need you there more than here,"* and I left as a soldier going to war. I knew that it would be for a short time and my life on this earth will be short-lived. If I stay here another 50 to 100 years, it is short compared to eternity. I have said to many people here on earth, that I want to live to be at least 95. I want to be a part of this unit here on earth as long as I can. I know what the heart of God is. It is to get people saved. It is to get people to live with Him forever.

God's Army On Earth

I also came to understand what the earthly unit looks like. First of all, this unit loves God with all their being. These are they that say Jesus is Lord and Savior. Not just Savior of their lives, but also Lord. They know they are sent out. They know who sent them. These have come to an understanding of His authority and whose authority they have. They know there is a war going on with Satan and his fallen angels. They know their weapons and use them in battles they encounter.

They have a great understanding of whose government and kingdom they are under and belong to. They spend a lot of time with the Father in His Word (Bible) and prayer. By doing this they are able to hear His commandment, when He commands them to do something. They understand that when Jesus or the Father through the Holy Spirit asks them to do something for the Kingdom, it is a command and not a request. These have come to know their purpose on this earth and accept it. They know that they are to get people to know Jesus as Lord and Savior at all cost. They are willing to lose their lives here on earth for Him. They know that they are part of a bigger army and have a God that will not leave them alone.

I came to understand that I was not being sent out alone with a heavy load. I understood that someone prayed me into the Kingdom of God. I also understood that God used both the heavenly, and the earthly units to have that accomplished in my life, and I know that those reading this that are saved - He did the same thing for you!

You that are reading this and are not saved, He is having the heavenly unit fight on your behalf. He is using me and anyone else in the earthly unit on your behalf.

I say to you: "Stop right now, and ask Jesus to be your Lord and Savior. Say the following prayer and know how much God loves you."

Prayer For Salvation

I know I have sinned. I am sorry for my sin. I believe, Jesus, that you died on the cross for my sin. I now receive you, Jesus, as my own Savior and Lord. With your help Jesus, I will try to please you everyday of my life. I will be a great soldier of honor in your army. In Jesus' name, Amen.

Chapter 12

Over 600 Heard Of Dean's Miracle Through Email

❖

The following emails were sent announcing my condition. This email went out to people I worked with, or for, at the time of the incident. It was also sent out to other departments throughout King County and the City of Seattle. It was sent to many of the different social agencies that I had worked with. In all, it can be said that this incident was announced to over 600 people. So when I showed up back to work a month and a half later, people could only say it was a miracle. I would then let them know it was a miracle performed by Jesus Christ and our Father God.

First Email

May 10, 2006
Hi Everyone,

This is a Wednesday update on Dean Braxton, beloved Manager of Juvenile Drug Court, and Treatment Court. As most all of you know by now, Dean had emergency surgery for kidney stones last Friday, May 5th, at St. Francis Hospital in Federal Way. Due to an infection and many other complications following the surgery, Dean's heart, kidneys and other vital organs began to shut down and he was placed on life support. He was transported on Saturday morning to Tacoma General Hospital ICU. He remains on life support, including a ventilator, 24/7 kidney dialysis, etc. He has made some progress in recovery and response over the past 3 days. He is receiving excellent care by the ICU medical team.

Currently, medical staffers are monitoring his heart, kidneys, and other functions and have addressed the white blood count problem that was discovered yesterday. His levels are returning to a more normal white count. They have had to increase his oxygen levels, however. This means he cannot breathe on his own. Although he cannot speak due to the ventilator, he is responding with facial expressions and tears when his wife and elderly parents speak with him. That is a good sign regarding his brain functioning and the wonderful spirit inside of Dean. We are continuing to pray for his complete recovery.

Dean's wife, Marilyn Braxton, would like to thank everyone for his or her kind visits, cards, telephone calls and other expressions of care and concern. She would like to request, however, that during this very critical time that Dean is on life-support, that all visits to Dean would be put on hold and all telephone calls to her would also be limited. Ycaza and Hazel from the 4Cs Coalition will be the main point people that I will be keeping updated through, as they are both very close to Marilyn and Dean and talking to her often.

We have arranged to have some food and beverages delivered to the family this week and we will keep you all posted on what is needed along the way. During this time of crisis, the family is spending very little time at home, so the needs are somewhat different.

Thank you for your loving care and concern, your offers of support and your continued prayers for Dean's healing and recovery. It is encouraging to all of us and to his family.

I will be in touch again soon,
Susie

Second Email

May 11, 2006
Good Morning Everyone,

This is a Thursday morning update on Dean Braxton: Marilyn Braxton reports that Dean is improving significantly at all levels. They are having conversations and other communication that shows to you the level of his improvement! Many miracles are unfolding and the ICU team at Tacoma General Hospital continues to be doing a superb job of caring for him.

Marilyn, Dean and their extended family want to express their continued gratefulness for your loving support, prayers and concern. They are encouraged by Dean's progress and want to pass along that encouragement to you. There is a road ahead to recovery, and it is great to report his movement along this road!

Dean will remain in ICU for a time because of the many issues involved in his care. I will keep you posted as I receive word from Marilyn through Hazel of the 4Cs Coalition about Dean's status and if he is moved to a regular room at the hospital.

Susie

Third Email

May 12, 2006

Good Afternoon Everyone,

This is a very encouraging update regarding Dean Braxton from his wife Marilyn. Over the past 24-30 hours, Dean has been making a remarkable recover, nothing short of miraculous, given the health crisis he has faced since last Friday just 1 week ago.

While he is still in the ICU at Tacoma General Hospital, he is improving by the hour, and is able to converse with his family and the medical staff.

His doctors are in awe of how quirky he has responded to treatment and how well he is doing.

Marilyn and the immediate family are with him much of the time and wanted to express their gratitude to all of you for your thoughts, prayers, and concerns for Dean. They are encouraged and grateful for the miracle of his recovery process.

It is unclear at this time how much longer Dean will be in ICU. There are many factors that must be addressed before he would move to a regular hospital room.

The family is still in need of gift cards for food. I will be taking a couple to them this evening. I would welcome any further donations any time during next week. I will be back in my office late Monday afternoon and part of Tuesday.

Thank again for your concern, prayers and support.

On behalf of the Drug Court/Treatment Court Teams,
Susie

Fourth Email

May 15, 2006

Hello Everyone,

I just spoke to Marilyn Braxton and Dean has been moved out of ICU, although he is still is at Tacoma General.

He is progressing every hour; she stated that he took a walk down the hall yesterday! She expressed her thanks for all the outpouring of love and support... And the doctors continue to be amazed at the rapid pace of recovery.

We are all encouraged keep the positive thoughts and prayers coming...

Susie

Fifth Email

May 16, 2006

Hi... Wasn't sure if you were included in yesterday's email from Margaret, Manager of Reclaiming Futures. Now that the team is back from their conference, Margaret or Mark will most likely provide the update information.

I was out sick yesterday, but spoke with Marilyn last evening. Dean is improving by the hour. It continues to be a miracle... Even to the doctors. At this point, he may be able to go home in a few days. He will still have recovering to do, but is almost well enough to do that at home! It's pretty much a WOW, isn't it!

Thanks for your thoughts and prayers for him,
Susie

Chapter 13

What Jesus Told Me About Our Churches

❖

When I was with Jesus, He looked at me and was downloading a great amount of information into my spirit
- the real me. The only way I can explain this process is like
a computer receiving information or being programmed with
information from another source, like what we call downloading information into a computer.

If you think about it, that is how Jesus communicates
information to all of us. Most people do not hear an audible
voice from Jesus. Most of the time we receive information
from Jesus like a computer being downloaded with information all at once. That is the same way he communicates with
all beings in heaven. So sharing information of my experience in heaven and what God said to me, is like me taking
apart a whole picture given to me at one time and giving it
out in pieces to others.

Now, I want to let you know what Jesus downloaded
into me about the churches here on earth and in the United
States.

Two Spirits In The Church

First, He let me know that there are two spirits (attitudes) in our churches today. You can find an appearance of both of these spirits or attitudes in Revelation 3:7-21. He said to me that these spirits are not of one denomination compared to another denomination. I used to think that way before I went to heaven. I have in the past, believed I was always in the right denomination and others were not. Whether I was with the Church of God in Christ, Southern Baptist, Assembly of God, Four Square and many non-denominational churches, I always believed my denomination was the right one. I believed we had the right spirit or attitude in the denomination I was in.

He let me know that His church is not one denomination against another. I came to realize that there are many things that we believe in that do not get us into heaven or keep us out. They keep us from helping others come to know Jesus as Lord and Savior. As long as someone follows Romans 10:9-10, they are in. What comes with this, is love for God and love for others. That causes changes in thinking and actions, but it is not one denomination over another. God just doesn't look at us that way.

We Are One Body

We do meet in different buildings, but He sees everyone who has accepted Jesus as Lord and Savor as His church. He also wants all of us to belong to a local body of believers so we can build each other up for the work He has set before us. There just were not any denominational lines in heaven. The many old jokes about denominations in heaven do not hold up, up there.

At the time I am writing this book, my wife and I do belong to a local body of believers. The name of the church is By His Word Christian Center in Tacoma, Washington. I came to understand that it is part of the government of God, that we belong to a local body of those who have made Jesus Lord and Savior of their lives. Jesus wants us to fellowship with others in His Kingdom.

Now the church as a whole has no denominational lines. What He said is that those two spirits are in every body of believers. Some bodies have more of one spirit than others. They can be in the same building of believers. Again, this changed how I look at churches all over this world. I came to know that every building that holds a church meeting has both of these spirits in it. One of these spirits can be stronger than the other in the same meeting. This is something that does not make Jesus happy. He is not happy when we esteem one church believing body (those who believe Jesus is Lord and Savior) over another church believing body. We are all part of the same church. I am talking about those who believe in Jesus as the Son of God and have made Him Lord and Savior of their lives. People that believe, that God the Father, sent His son into the world to save it, to save you, to save people. Those that believe the Holy Spirit, Jesus and the Father are one and that there is only one true God, the one who made man, not a man made God.

He let me know that He has His children in these believing bodies, meeting in a number of buildings and denominations. Everyone who believes that Jesus is the Christ has been fathered by God (1John 5:1).

He went on to let me know that He still has His children in those other church believing bodies or denominations. He wants us to stop tearing each other down. He is still working with all of us. He wants us to follow His Government/ Kingdom rules on how to confront, correct or deal with each other.

The First Spirit

The first spirit is found in Revelation 3:8-12, the church of Philadelphia explains this spirit.

Revelation 3:8-12 (NKJV)
"I know your works. See, I have set before you an
open door, and no one can shut it for you have a
little strength, have kept My word, and have not
denied My name. Indeed I will make those of the
synagogue of Satan, who say they are Jews and are
not, but lie—indeed I will make them come and
worship before your feet, and to know that I have
loved you. Because you have kept My command
to persevere, I also will keep you from the hour
of trial which shall come upon the whole world,
to test those who dwell on the earth. Behold, I am
coming quickly! Hold fast what you have, that no
one may take your crown. He who overcomes, I
will make him a pillar in the temple of My God,
and he shall go out no more. I will write on him
the name of My God and the name of the city of
My God, the New Jerusalem, which comes down
out of heaven from My God. And I will write on
him My new name.

This spirit has the will to serve others first. Those who
have this spirit keep God's Word at all cost. They have not
denied His Name. They also know His Word is the Word
of perseverance, in which He keeps them from the hour of
testing. Those who hold on to this spirit know in their heart
that He is coming quickly.

They understand it is quick to them because they want to
see more people saved. They are holding fast to what they
know. Those that have this spirit have a crown that no one
can take from them, they can give it away, but no one can
take it. They are truly overcoming all that they face on this
earth. They will be made a pillar in God's temple and will
not go out from the temple of God. They will have the name

of God written on them along with the name of the city of God on them.

Again, this spirit is in all of those bodies that believe in Jesus Christ as Lord and Savior.

The Second Spirit

The second spirit or attitude is found in Revelation 3:15-21 and was in the Laodicean church.

Revelation 3:15-21 (NKJV)
"I know your works, that you are neither cold nor hot. I could wish you were cold or hot. So then, because you are lukewarm, and neither cold nor hot, I will vomit you out of My mouth. Because you say, 'I am rich, have become wealthy, and have need of nothing' - and do not know that you are wretched, miserable, poor, blind, and naked - I counsel you to buy from Me gold refined in the fire, that you may be rich; and white garments, that you may be clothed, that the shame of your nakedness may not be revealed; and anoint your eyes with eye salve, that you may see. As many as I love, I rebuke and chasten. Therefore be zealous and repent. Behold, I stand at the door and knock. If anyone hears My voice and opens the door, I will come in to him and dine with him, and he with Me. To him who overcomes I will grant to sit with Me on My throne, as I also overcame and sat down with My Father on His throne.

This is the spirit I did not want to have any part with. At the time of this incident I believed that any traditional building church was as the Laodicean's church. I was pastoring a small home church at the time and very happy with it. I had been a part of the traditional church for a number of years as you have already read, and most of those years as an assistant pastor. Because of some of the experiences I had in some of those churches I did not want to have anything to do with them. The older the denomination, the more as the Laodiceans I believed they were. But as I stated before, that has changed for me. I came to know it has nothing to do with a building or a denomination. It has everything to do with a person's heart.

This spirit is neither cold or hot. It does not work for God. These people who call themselves believers in Jesus are not on the side of God. Jesus said He wished they were either cold or hot. Because they are lukewarm He is going to spit (Greek: vomit) them out of His mouth. They that have this spirit say they are rich, wealthy and need nothing. They may not say it out loud so others can hear them, but in their heart they believe this. Their problem is that God knows their heart, and He knows which spirit they have.

Jesus said they do not know they are wretched, miserable, poor, blind and naked. Then Jesus goes on to tell them to buy gold from Him, that has been refined by fire. He wants them to be truly rich. He wants them to have white garments so they can clothe themselves. He does not want the shame of their nakedness to be revealed. He wants them to have their eyes to be opened so they can see. Because HE LOVES THEM, he reproves and disciplines them who have this spirit. He wants them to be zealous and repent from this spirit. Jesus is knocking on the door to their spirit, waiting for them to open their spirit to Him. He wants to come into their spirit and dine with them and they with Him. Those who repent and overcome this lukewarm state will sit down with Jesus on His throne.

I came to understand that those who are lukewarm are in every body of believers, no matter what building they meet in or what denomination they belong to, He is reaching out to them. Do not be deceived like I was. He loves them so much that He will keep knocking until they open up or die. I was one of those lukewarm people for a long time, and He did not give up on me. He does not want us to give up on them either.

The Church Can Change Our Nations

The other thing He downloaded into me is *"How the church down here on earth goes, so does a nation."* If we see a problem in our nation we must first look at our churches. He really does want His people who are called by His name to humble themselves, pray, seek His face and turn from their individual wicked ways. This always turns a nation around. We that believe in Jesus as Lord and Savior, can change our nations around, whether it is the United States, Peru, France, England, Canada, China, Uganda, Israel, or your nation. He wants us to know it can happen. We can change the earth to get more people saved.

2 Chronicles 7:14 (NKJV)
if My people who are called by My name will humble themselves, and pray and seek My face, and turn from their wicked ways, then I will hear from heaven, and will forgive their sin and heal their land.

Chapter 14

What God Does With Our Prayers

One Day I'll Be Home
It was as if my skin didn't fit
But I had just realized it
Feeling like a stranger
In a place I had always called home.

But then I heard your voice
It was as if a light bulb went off
And I just knew
That was where I belonged

It was as if I had just met someone
But knew them for ages
Every line, every feature
Every eccentricity

It was as if every awkwardness
Just melted away
Every pain, every humiliation
Every feeling of not enough

It was as if someone had dug
Into the deepest recess of my heart
And found what I had been longing for
My home

It was as if every childhood dream
Every feeling of rightness
Every good memory, every hope
Was heard in your words

It was as if I already knew you
You were describing my home
You knew my home
One day I'll be home
By Teresa Smith

2 Corinthians 5:8 (NKJV)
**...to be absent from the body and to be present
with the Lord.**

It was great to be traveling to where Jesus is. I was moving very fast. I did not see anyone when I left. I was not looking for anyone else but Jesus. I knew where I was going. On the way back to my body I did see demons in that thick blackness that surrounds our galaxies. As I got close to the hospital, I saw the Doctors and Nurse working on me in the hospital room. However, when I left my body, I was not looking back. I knew where to go and no one had to tell me where to go. I did not need any direction. I did not need an angel taking me. I knew I was going home and I was to be at the feet of Jesus.

Now as I said, I was moving super fast. As 2 Corinthians says, I was absent from my body, and was in the presence of my Lord. I was moving faster than it takes you to read the next sentence. I was absent from my body and was in the presence of my Lord. If I were to die right now, I would be in heaven in a twinkling of an eye. Yet the prayers of people that were praying for me and other prayers were moving faster than I was. They were like shooting stars passing me. All I saw as they went by me were balls that looked like fire and a tail of light that looked like fire. I saw prayers as I was going to heaven and prayers as I was coming back to the hospital on earth. I was moving in a river of prayers going to heaven. The prayers close to me were for me, the farther away the prayers were from me, they were for other people.

Just think, if you were praying at the time I left my body to go to heaven I saw your prayer pass me by. They passed me as if I was standing still. Yet, to be absent from my body I was in the presence of my Lord.

Two Types Of Prayers

I knew there were two types of prayers passing me. One type were prayers from people that had prayed a prayer and understood the authority they had when they prayed the prayer. They were praying in faith from their hearts. They were praying according to a verse in the Bible that they had understood the meaning of. They were praying the will of God over me and others. So when they prayed it, they knew in their heart what it was supposed to do. And they knew that God would answer the prayer with His power. John tells us about this kind of prayer.

1 John 5:14-15 (NKJV)
Now this is the confidence that we have in Him, that if we ask anything according to His will, He hears us. And if we know that He hears us, whatever we ask, we know that we have the petitions that we have asked of Him.

Now I had no problem with this kind of prayer. We are told to pray His will here on earth in Matthew 6:10. I study to know His will according to the Bible, so this prayer did not surprise me.

This was the prayer my wife was praying along with my children and others. It was God's will for me to come back to this earth. Since it was His will it was answered. But also remember my wife's sacrifice and battle to get that outcome. That was God's will.

The other prayer was a surprise to me. It was a prayer that I never thought exists. This was one of the box-blowing moments for me (think outside of the box). It was a prayer that people had prayed that they really did not have the full understanding of what they were praying. They did not doubt what they were praying. They just did not understand the full impact of what they had asked for. They were on the right track to understanding the will of God in an area, but did not fully understand it yet. They had faith in what they prayed, not really understanding what they were fully praying for. Yet, God honored the prayer as if they understood the power of what they had asked.

Again, they did not doubt what they were praying for, but had faith for all they understood. I like to say that they believed they were praying for something that would produce a bang as big as a firecracker and God would honor their prayer as a nuclear bomb. He was going to answer the prayer as if they understood the full impact of what they were praying about. You see this best in little children. I have seen a child pray for something and as far as they know, it is done. They may know very little about the Bible, but they do know about God. You can find this prayer in Ephesians.

Ephesians 3:20 (NKJV)
Now to Him who is able to do exceedingly abun-
dantly above all that we ask or think, according to
the power that works in us

Where Our Prayers Go

Now as I said before, I went to the feet of Jesus and stopped there. The prayers went straight to the throne and the Father. Not only did they go to the Father God, they went inside of Him. To try to understand this you will have to understand that the throne of God is not a seat. It is a place. Well, more than that, He is the Throne. I will cover the Throne of God in this book later. But for now, I need to continue with what happens to the prayers we pray.

There were millions upon millions of prayers entering the Father. Our prayers became Him and He became our prayers. I saw these lights of prayers like shooting stars entering the Father. I came to understand that He answers our prayers with Himself.

At first, when I came back to earth and someone asked me about prayers I had a hard time telling them what I saw. This again, was outside of my boxes. I remembered praying to the Father asking Him how would I explain this. How do I explain seeing the prayers of people here on earth enter God?

When He directed me to Exodus, I found the answer to explain the prayers going into the Father.

Exodus 3:13-14 (NKJV)
Then Moses said to God, "Indeed, when I come
to the children of Israel and say to them, 'The
God of your fathers has sent me to you,' and they
say to me, 'What is His name?' what shall I say
to them?" And God said to Moses, "I AM WHO

I AM." And He said, "Thus you shall say to the children of Israel, 'I AM has sent me to you."

The Lord says here - I AM. HE IS THE ANSWER TO OUR PRAYERS! He does answer our prayers with Himself.

Why did He come? Why did He come to the children of Israel? God tells us in Exodus 3:7-9 why He came.

Exodus 3:7-9 (NKJV)
And the LORD said: "I have surely seen the oppression of My people who are in Egypt, and have heard their cry because of their taskmasters, for I know their sorrows. "So I have come down to deliver them out of the hand of the Egyptians, and to bring them up from that land to a good and large land, to a land flowing with milk and honey, to the place of the Canaanites and the Hittites and the Amorites and the Perizzites and the Hivites and the Jebusites. "Now therefore, behold, the cry of the children of Israel has come to Me, further-more, and I have also seen the oppression with which the Egyptians oppress them.

The Israelites were praying for a deliverer, a savior, and a healer. The prayers went into the Father God and he became their answer. He became their deliverer, their savior, and their healer. Just as He is our answer to any prayer we have prayed to Him, He is our savior, joy, peace, righteousness, and so on. Right now just say it - "God is my answer to any problem I have and He wants to be!"

Our God Is!

He truly is the answer to our prayers, which is why we call Him:

- **JEHOVAH-JIREH**: Jehovah will see; i.e., will provide, the name given by Abraham to the scene of his offering up the ram which was caught in the thicket on Mount Moriah. The expression used in Lord provides." It is said to this day, "In the mountain of the Lord provision will be made." in the mount of the Lord it shall be seen," has been regarded as equal to the saying, "Man's extremity is God's opportunity." (Gen. 22:8, 14)
- **JEHOVAH-NISSI**: Jehovah my banner, the title given by Moses to the altar which he erected on the hill on the top of which he stood with uplifted hands while Israel prevailed over their enemies the Amalekites (Ex. 17:15 Lord is my Banner)
- **JEHOVAH-SHALOM**: Yahweh is peace. This was the name given by Gideon to the altar he built at Ophra, in allusion to the word spoken to him by the Lord, "Peace be unto thee" (Judg 6:24)
- **JEHOVAH-SHAMMAH**: Jehovah is there, the symbolical title given by Ezekiel to Jerusalem, which was seen by him in vision. The name of the city from that day forward will be The Lord Is There. It was a type of the gospel Church. (Ezek. 48:35)
- **JEHOVAH-TSIDCKENU**: Jehovah our righteousness, rendered in the Authorized Version, "The LORD our righteousness," a title given to the Messiah. Judah will enjoy safety and Israel will live in security. This is the name he will go by: The Lord has provided us with justice. And also to Jerusalem (Jer 23:6, 33:16)

Whatever the need you have, He is the answer. The Bible tells us this and it is true.

Prayers From The Heart

As you read earlier, Jesus downloaded information into me. He downloaded information in me about prayers. I understood that our prayers must come from our heart. Our God is a heart God, and He is looking for us to talk to Him from our heart. I do not have the word yet to describe this, but our prayers become substances. What kind of substance? I do not have words to describe. They only become substances if we are praying to God from our heart. He hears us if we are praying from our heart. This is why most little children receive their requests. In Romans 10:9 God is looking at the heart.

Romans 10:9 (NKJV)
that if you confess with your mouth the Lord Jesus and believe in your heart that God raised Him from the dead, you will be saved.

He hears your heart. He understands your heart. He only hears prayers from the heart. Some ask, "What if your heart is wrong when you pray?" The Holy Spirit will let you know. It is up to you to listen to Him. He will also help you to pray from your heart. The Holy Spirit came to help us do a lot of things right; the way God wants them done. Prayer is one of those things.

Luke 11:13 (NKJV)
"If you then, being evil, know how to give good gifts to your children, how much more will your heavenly Father give the Holy Spirit to those who ask Him!"

Matthew 7:11 (NKJV)
"If you then, being evil, know how to give good gifts to your children, how much more will your

Father who is in heaven give good things to those who ask Him!

Read Luke 11:1-13 to understand what happens to the prayers we pray from the heart.

People have asked, "How do I know if I am praying His will?" My reply to them is, "Ask Him to help you pray from your heart." I know He hears you because that is His will. You can read that again in 1John 5:14-15. They pray from the heart. After you ask Him from your heart, you do not have to ask Him again. He heard you. God is not hard of hearing or remembering, but we pray to Him as if He is.

I understood that our prayers do not need to be repeated if they are asked from the heart, and that our Father does not forget a prayer that is asked from the heart. We may forget our prayers, but He does not. A person asked me one time, "What if I did not pray right? Do I have to ask it again?" I replied, "You can if you want, but God listens to your heart. If you are asking from the heart He hears you. You have your request. Now thank Him."

Prayers Don't Have A Shelf Life

Another thing I came to understand about prayer is that if it is a prayer from the heart, it does not have a shelf life. God does not forget your prayers. He remembers them until they are answered. It could be within minutes, hours, days, years, or even longer. But, your prayers do not expire. There is not an expiration date on them.

This means that those prayers you keep on praying over and over for someone to get saved, He heard you the first time and as soon as that person turns their heart toward God, God will be there to meet that person. All you need to do now is thank Him. He wants your loved ones to be saved more than you do. Remember, the Father gave his Son, Jesus, so that they could be saved. So thank Him for hearing your prayer and your prayer being answered. It does not matter if you see it answered here on earth or when you are in heaven. Wherever you are, you will rejoice.

My mother did not make Jesus her Lord and Savior over her life until ten years after my grandmother Mary, her mother, had died. I know when my mother made that step my grandmother Mary rejoiced over my mother's salvation.

Some of you that are reading this right now, are answers to prayer someone prayed a long time ago. Some of you are answers to a prayer some great, great, great, great, grandparent prayed for you. They prayed for a great, great, great, great grandchild to know Jesus as Lord and Savior. And since there is no expiration date, when you turned your heart to God, their prayer was answered.

Some of you have prayers that were prayed over you by someone a long time ago that God is waiting to answer. You just need to get your heart right. Ask Jesus to help you.

Here is one more thing I must say about what I learned about prayer. Our prayers cause movement in the Kingdom of God. Jesus is strategizing by how we pray. In the Bible we can read that we are to pray for the Lord to send laborers into His harvest in Matthew 9:37-38.

Jesus Giving Out Orders

When I saw Jesus strategizing, He knelt down to the ground and put His hand out pointing at the ground and the ground rose up and became a city. What city? I could not tell you. I just knew it was an earthly city. He pointed at areas in the city and looked up at a being (angel). They would bow, and back out fast. I knew He had given them instruction on what to do. I knew that Jesus had received information about a situation on earth that the Father had gotten from someone praying here on earth and gave that information to Jesus at the same moment He had received the information. Then Jesus saw what the Father wanted and gave that information to the angel, and he would leave to go to the earth. They would carry out the orders that were given to them by Jesus. You can also read about this in Daniel 10:12. I know that my wife put this into action from earth when she prayed the will of God. She acted on Matthew 6:10 and Luke 11:2

Matthew 6:10 (NKJV)
Your kingdom come. Your will be done On earth as it is in heaven.

Luke 11:2 (NKJV)
So He said to them, "When you pray, say: Our Father in heaven, Hallowed be Your name. Your kingdom come. Your will be done On earth as it is in heaven."

So, as you can read we are told to pray the will of heaven here on earth. This is what I saw when I was there. God's will being performed in heaven to be played out here on earth.

Another thing that must be said loud and clear is that we have the only God who hears prayer. Sometimes we act if there are a number of gods in heaven and ours is just one of them. This is not true. I saw only one God, and He was not sharing His Throne with anyone else. Not Mohammed, Buddha or any other so-called religious figure. Now, the Father God who sits on the Throne and Jesus the son of God, were the only one receiving praise from the creation of God in heaven. No other being or creation of God was getting, receiving or giving praise to any other but the Father and Jesus.

There is only one God who can hear prayer and answer it clear around the world. No other so-called god can. But we must understand that there is only one God, and one God who hears prayers. WE MUST BELIEVE THAT! As I said before, we pray to the God who made man, not a god made by man.

Chapter 15

I Saw God The Father On His Throne And His Love For Us!

You Did This For Me
From the beginning of time
From the Old testament to the New
Stories were written of a place
Where there were no worries or cares
There are streets of gold
Musical notes springing from waterfalls of crystal
Lights that shine brighter than the sun
On the hottest summer day
Every color imaginable shine
From the crystal edges of His crown
His robe of the purest white
Draped over His golden brass colored feet
Songs of praise and worship to the Father filled the
    open sky
As the spirits danced thankful for favor, grace and
    mercy
Kneeling down at the feet of our brother Jesus Christ
A light beamed from the palms of both His hands

Uttered from my lips these five words:
You did this for me!
By Dorothea Elisha Holmes

As I said earlier, I saw the prayers people were praying for me and the prayers of others entering God the Father on His Throne. I want to attempt to describe Father God as I saw Him there in heaven.

God the Father is as the Bible says, a Spirit. He is pure SPIRIT. He is pure LOVE. He is pure LIFE. And He is pure LIGHT. That is who He is. If only we could understand that in our interpretation of the Bible. I tell people that this understanding of who God is, gave me a better understanding of what I read in the Bible. I connect everything that God does back to who He is. Love, Life and Light. He cannot come at us any other way than what He is. All that He does comes out of who He is. He is love, just like John tells us in the Bible. He is the true Spirit and we must worship Him in spirit and truth. He is pure light that is still expanding. He is life.

I heard all of creation, but those who have been redeemed refer to the Father God as the WORD. He is His Word and His Word is Him. They would say, "The Word said..."

Now, those of us who are redeemed would call Him Father. We are truly His children and we refer to Him as Father. This is good news. We who are redeemed are the only ones who call Him Father.

What Does The Father Look Like?

I have had this question asked many times, "What does the Father look like?" They ask if He looks human. He is vast. He is very vast. The word "big" does not come close to describing what I saw, or experienced. The angels that fly around Him saying, "holy, holy, holy" to Him, are very small compared to God.

He has the form of a human. Or better yet, we have the form of God. We look like Him. We were made after His likeness. I really cannot put my thinking around Him. He is large, huge, vast, infinite, enormous, immeasurable, unrestricted, unrestrained, never ending, endless, without end, free and at liberty to be God. I like to say the word "vast", mostly because the word comes out of my mouth in such a way that there is no ending. I really have not found words in English to describe God. I have no thought to even grasp what I saw. When I try to put Him in my thinking, I can't. If I think of the beginning of Him I lose the end and if I think of the end I lose the beginning. One time, I thought on this for a little while and knew if I kept trying to place God inside of my thinking, I was going to end up with a headache. So I just don't try it anymore. You that know Jesus as Lord and Savior, you will see Him and see what I am saying. All I can say is that He is vast.

There is no end to God the Father. He is bright like Jesus with many colors coming off of Him. Jesus and the Father God light up everything. They do not let any darkness in heaven. None at all! Every being there has God the Father and Jesus inside of them. They live outside of every being and inside every being. Every being shines because of the Father God and Jesus. They are the light within every living being and creature. Darkness has nowhere to hide.

I am coming way short in telling you about the Father. Jesus was easier to describe only because He has a new body. We that know Jesus as Lord and Savior will someday have that same body He has.

The Father's Throne

I saw the Father God sitting on the Throne and again, one of my boxes was blown up. He was sitting on the throne and He is the Throne. As I said earlier, He had these colors coming off of Him, more colors than I can tell you. The colors that came off of Him were alive. Everything that comes from God the Father is alive.

Before the Throne, there was an uncountable number of heavenly creatures giving God praise. Later, I will go into more detail of this praise before the Throne of God.

Now, I will try to describe the Throne of God. This is what I saw: God was vast and the Throne was God, and God was the Throne. He was in the midst of the Throne and connected to the Throne. Where He was, the Throne was there. The Throne was bright and looked like a cloud. I had always believed God was sitting on a chair, but that was not so. This is one of my boxes that was blown up. The throne looked like a cloud.

What I experienced about the Throne was that God the Father was and has never been separated from the Throne. When I talk about the Throne, it has been hard for me to take in all that I experienced before the Throne of God. God says in Isaiah that, *"Heaven is My Throne and the earth is My footstool."*

Isaiah 66:1-2 (NKJV)
Thus says the Lord: "Heaven is My throne, and the earth is My footstool. Where is the house that you will build Me? And where is the place of My rest? "For all those things My hand has made, and all those things exist," says the Lord.

Acts 7:48-50 (NKJV)
"However, the Most High does not dwell in temples made with hands, as the prophet says: "Heaven is My throne, and earth is My footstool. What house will you build for Me? says the Lord, "Or what is the place of My rest? Has My hand not made all these things?"

Matthew 5:34 (NKJV)
"But I say to you, do not swear at all: neither by
heaven, for it is God's throne.

This Throne which was God Himself, is all I could come back with to tell others of what I saw. The throne of God is not what I used to believe it was. I only could say to myself after seeing God on the Throne, in the midst of the Throne, and being the Throne, "Who could make a Throne for God, but God?" And it was not like what a human would make.

Our Father's Love For Us

As I looked at the Throne, I saw how much the Father loves us. I knew Jesus loved us so much, but to see the Father's love for us - WOW! I looked in His eyes. When I did, all I could think was, "I don't know how many universes you can place in His eyes." But out of all that I saw, what really stood out to me was the love that He has for each and every one of us on earth.

I came to understand that every time we take a breath of air, the Father God is saying, "I love you." The only reason air is here, is for you. There is no other reason that the air is here. How many times in a day do you take a breath of air? Whatever the number is, is how many times God is telling you that He loves you. Hear Him as you breathe say, *"I Love you."*

We Are All Number One

I understood that there is no number two in God's eyes. Everyone is number one. There is no one taking the place of number two, three, four, five, six, seven, eight, nine, or the tenth person. There is only number one, everyone is number one to Him. Everyone is first in line with Him. There is no difference even here on earth. If you know Jesus as Lord and

Savior you are number one to Him. As the Bible says, we are
the apple of His eye.

Psalm 17:8 (NKJV)
Keep me as the apple of Your eye; Hide me under
the shadow of Your wings

Zechariah 2:8 (NKJV)
For thus says the LORD of hosts: "He sent Me
after glory, to the nations which plunder you;
for he who touches you touches the apple of His
eye."

I came to know how valuable we are to Him:

John 3:16-17 (NKJV)
For God so loved the world that He gave His only
begotten Son, that whoever believes in Him should
not perish but have everlasting life. For God did
not send His Son into the world to condemn the
world, but that the world through Him might be
saved.

Received Back From The Dead

Received back from the dead, you have blessed us
by the Glory you have seen and by what you have said.
Marvelously touching both heaven and earth,
what you experienced is truly a second re-birth.
You encourage us to stay true to God's Word,
to walk the talk and live the way that we should.
We cover you with our brotherly prayers,
that God keeps you free from burdens and cares,
or other distractions and worldly strife
that might hinder God's plan for your Spirit-led life.

Stay in that place, transformed in the Lord,
transformed to the Word, a place you have shared,
a place that's so good!
We are stirred up to desire it with the whole of our
     heart,
that each day we awake to a fresh and new start.
You've helped us see God through sparkling new eyes,
raising new awareness and new heart cries
that kindles new passion and greater desire
to stay close to the Lord in His refining love's fire.
Amen
By Nancy Greco

Chapter 16

Worship Before
The Throne Of God

❖

As I said earlier, I saw the Father God sitting on His Throne with an uncountable number of heavenly creatures before the Throne giving God praise. I was on my hands and knees when I looked at the Throne of God.

This is what I saw: I was far and yet I was near the Throne of God. As I told you, there were countless numbers of beings around the Throne. Some had been human beings from earth and others were heavenly beings. Between them and the Throne was something like water. John said in Revelations that it was like a crystal sea. It looks like crystal, but it is not. It is something like water but not really. The closest I can come to describing this water-like substance is by calling it water. But again, it is like water and it is very much alive.

Now after this Crystal-like Sea there was another liquid under the throne of God. The throne hovers over this liquid and this liquid was also alive. It had a different thickness to it compared to the Crystal-like Sea. These two liquids flowed through each other, but did not overlap or blend or bleed into each other. They stay very much separate. I have not found the words to really describe the beauty of both of these water-like liquids. All I can say is that they were alive and they had a personality to them. Throughout heaven there are more water-like liquids that are alive and have a fun personality.

At the moment I was in heaven there always seemed to be a sound of praise and worship. I came to understand that true worship is doing God's will. So in the atmosphere there was always what seemed to be like a musical sound. It was going on all the time and yet it was like no other sound that I know of. It was more than just hearing it. It was like you experienced it. The closest I can come to describing it is like a drum beat. Vibrations that you can feel or the bass coming from another car next to yours. This praise was always there in the atmosphere.

There was also a sound of praise and worship you could hear. Just before I saw what was happening before the Throne of God, all of what we would call sound, stopped. It was quiet. Everything got really quiet. There was no noise at all. I came to know what quiet is. We always have noise going on around us here on earth. Even when we think it is quiet, there is always some sound going on around us. At that moment I did not hear a thing.

The Heavenly Worship Leader

The next thing I saw was one of the beings before the Throne rising up from a kneeling position. This being rose up like an elevator rising up from the bottom floor to the top slowly. This being was so beautiful. This being looked liked a woman but I knew it was not. It was a good hundred stories or higher. When it reached its highest point, this being rose its arms over its head to the full extent and extended its fingers out wide. The color of this being was light blue, like the sky on a sunny day. It seemed as if you could see through this being, but it was hard to tell for the rainbow color was coming off of God entering into the being.

After this being had finished rising, it opened its mouth and broke the silence that was taking place. It started to sing in a language I understood but knew was not an earthly language. This language seemed to be this being's own language, but I understood it. The sound that came out of its mouth was beautiful and yet, just one note. It came from the innermost part of its being. This being seemed to be making music within itself. This is how all the beings produce music.

Musical Instruments Inside "The Being"

After being back on earth someone asked me about the music in heaven. I told them about how I heard and saw music coming out of the beings in heaven. After telling this to this person for the first time, I said within myself, "Dean, you have really gone off." But I knew I had to tell what I saw, whether they believed me or not. Whether I had believed this before or not, I had to tell the truth since they had asked. I had never heard anyone tell me that angels in heaven had instruments inside of themselves. That was the first time I said something that I had not known was in the Bible, but it would not be the last time. Later, I found out that Lucifer, or now Satan, was created with instruments inside him.

Ezekiel 28:13 (NKJV)
You were in Eden, the garden of God; Every precious stone was your covering: The sardius, topaz, and diamond, Beryl, onyx, and jasper, Sapphire, turquoise, and emerald with gold. The workmanship of your timbrels and pipes was prepared for you on the day you were created.
(KJV reads: IN THEE in the day that thou wast created.)

Timbrels or tabrets: Greek word toph, Pronunciation: tofe Definition: 1) timbrel, tambourine. Origin: taphaph, Pronunciation: taw-faf, Definition: 1) to play or sound the timbrel, beat, play upon, drum (on a timbrel or other object)

Pipes: Greek word neqeb Pronunciation: neh'keb, Definition: 1) groove, socket, hole, cavity, settings 1a) technical term relating to jeweler's work

The Sound Of Music In Heaven

Now the notes that were coming out of this beautiful being were one note at a time. This being started with a high note and then would go to a low note, then come back to a high note but lower than the previous high note before. Then go back to a low note but higher than the previous low note before. The notes seemed to be layered on top of each other. The high notes on another high note and the lower notes on another lower note. As this being would go from high to low it sped up the movement between high and low notes. It was moving between each note faster and faster. I had the ability to follow each note as it left the being, no matter how fast they were coming out of the being. I could see the notes coming out of the being's mouth. They had substance to them. Substance that I have not found anything here on earth to compare to what the notes were made out of. They were on top of each other. You could hold them and walk on them. You could hear and experience each note that came out of this being's mouth.

This being kept singing and producing music until it filled the atmosphere with the sounds of these notes. These notes finally ended up entering the Father on the Throne. I could hear the sounds even as I was leaving heaven. I could hear the sounds even after I left heaven. I hear them even now. When this being finally reached an apex or top of praise, the being stopped and bowed back on its knees, like slowly going down in an elevator.

What was this beautiful being doing? For a long time after, I would try to sing the music I heard in heaven. I've tried to hum the sounds and toot the sounds. I would try anything that would produce music to get the sounds out of my head. It was not that the sounds were driving me crazy, I just wanted everyone to hear what I had heard in heaven.

I would even try to get those who produce music to construct some of the sounds. They all came up way short, because of the boxes (rules) they place music in. I started to realize that I wouldn't be able to get this music out until I came in contact with the right person or persons.

He Hit The Note!

I was in Creswell, Oregon talking to a church about heaven. The people who had invited us had a little gathering the day before, for us to hear this person from Korea who played the violin. As he was playing, he was coming close to some of the sounds I heard in heaven. They were mostly the sounds I heard from the beautiful light blue being. I asked him if we could find time to see what we could get out of my head in the ways of these sounds. So Sunday after church I sat down with him. He started to play different notes on his violin. As he got closer to the first note that came out of the being's mouth I got excited. Then he hit the note that I first heard come out of the being. I stopped him and said, "That is it! That is it!"

I asked him what note that was. He said the note A. Then he said in broken English, that it was amazing that I would recognize that note as the first note that came out of the being's mouth. Then he proceeded to tell me why he was amazed. He was a concert violinist that played in an orchestra. He said that in an orchestra before they start to play, he and others in the orchestra would tune up off the note A. Until everyone in the orchestra was on the same line as the note A, they would not start to play music. He was so amazed I could remember that note above all the others as the first note that came out of the being's mouth.

A Call To Worship

After we discussed this in more detail, I came to understand what this beautiful light blue being was doing. This being was having all the other creation of God tune up off the notes of A coming from its mouth. It was calling all of heaven to praise the Father and Jesus, which was this being's purpose. This being was connecting all of God's creation to praise God. It connected in sound of substance with each of God's creations in the power of its purpose to bring a sound of praise to God. This being produced notes of praise, in which each note was a full praise for God. Each note connected a heavenly creation to the praise of God the Father.

After the beautiful blue being was back on its knees, I could still hear the sounds that came out of its mouth as the rest of heaven started to praise God. For I saw to the right of me and to the right of the throne, a large multitude of beings came up as on a number of elevators off of their knees like the first being did.

The Multitude Of Beings

Some of them were heavenly beings and others had been human beings. The numbers were more than I could count. I knew that some of the heavenly beings had been there before the throne for what seemed to me, to be forever. Each being was shining and beautiful. All the redeemed (who had been human on earth) where shining and white as light, the others were all colors and shining.

They started to praise the Father. Each being was singing a love song to the Father, in its own language. I again, understood all the languages and each song was an individual love song to the Father. Each song sounded so wonderful, beautiful, lovely, and words I have not put a voice to. Again, I have tried to hum the sounds, toot the sounds, sing the sounds and I have not come close yet.

When one group was done, another group would rise up, or just one being would rise up. They would rise up off their knees to sing. Again, each note was made with substance. You could hold each note in your hand. Every note was praise in itself. Each being sang out of their innermost being.

This kept on happening over and over. These beings were rising up and bowing back down on their knees. They did not sound like they were harmonizing or, as a symphony or orchestra. I saw no instruments. I am not saying that there were no instruments in heaven, I just did not see any because I was experiencing the sounds coming out of each being. Each being seemed to need no instrument to make the sound of an instrument. Every beings' voice has a place in heaven. I came to understand that God has made a place in heaven for our voice, which no one can take away or replace. These voices did not clash when praising.

The Crystal-Like Sea's Part In Worship

Now I am about to open an area that few have seen and come back here on earth to tell about. I will not say it was outside of my boxes or thinking. I just did not even think of the things I saw in heaven as they praised God the Father before His Throne. Again, I just have to tell you what I saw.

After the notes of the multitude of beings left them, the notes seemed to dance as they rose to the Father on the Throne. Before they got to the Father, the Crystal-like Sea that was before the Throne rose up in the atmosphere and intercepted the notes and would make a hole in itself to have the notes dance through. This seemed to change the sound of the notes higher or lower, like blowing through a horn, flute or some other instrument. It was beautiful! The sounds that came out of the Crystal-like Sea were amazing. The Crystal-like Sea was playing the beings' notes like a person would play the piano. The Crystal-like Sea had been doing this for what seemed to me, forever.

Dancing In Heaven

The Crystal-like Sea also made movements in the atmosphere that praised the Father. What wonderful movements of love this Crystal-like Sea showed before the Father.

After the notes left the Crystal-like Sea into the atmosphere, the notes met up with the colors coming off of the Father. These colors were alive and would hold onto the notes and dance with them. The colors would dance with the notes all the way back up to the Father and let go, just before the notes would enter the Father.

What I noticed as I followed the notes passing through the Crystal-like Sea, as it was changing the sounds of the notes and praising the Father with a number of loops in the atmosphere and other movements, was that I saw another multitude of beings. Some heavenly beings, and some that had been human beings here on earth. These beings were dancing in praise to the Father on the Throne. They were in the atmosphere above the water. These beings were dancing in beautiful motions to the Father on the Throne.

Behind the dancing, in front of the dancing, below the dancing, and above the dancing of these beings - separating all of this, was the Crystal-like Sea, colors and notes.

The Thunders Of Heaven

The atmospheres were praising the Father on the Throne. It reminded me of the Fourth of July in the United States of America. How we here in the United States would have firecrackers explode in the atmosphere. The atmospheres were just popping all over the place in praise for the Father on the Throne. John, in Revelation 14:2, described it as thunder.

Revelation 14:2 (NKJV)
And I heard a voice from heaven, like the voice of
many waters, and like the voice of loud thunder.
And I heard the sound of harpists playing their
harps.

The Beings Flying Around The Father

Then there were the beings flying around the Father on the Throne. Living Creatures as John said in Revelations 4:6-7, 9 and seraphim as Isaiah called them in Isaiah 6:2-4. These were the beings flying around the Father on the Throne saying, "HOLY, HOLY, HOLY." There are more than one. I saw a multitude of them flying around the Father on the Throne. Some had what looked like eyes on their wings and others did not. What looked like eyes on the wings, would blink and something would come out of them in praise for the Father on the Throne.

Above the Father on His Throne is His glory. Just His wonderful glory. Within His glory, is His praise for Himself. Some of you will understand what I just said. Some of you will not. But no one can praise God more than God. For only God knows who He truly is. So His glory only, can praise Him.

This Worship Has Changed My Life

All of what I told you here really falls short of all I saw before the Throne of God. I have not had the question come my way to tell more and yet, there is a lot more that takes place before the Throne of God. All I can say is that those of you that know Jesus as Lord and Savior will see all I have tried to disclose to you here and more.

As I saw and listened to this worship before my Father's Throne, I heard a sound so beautiful that it has changed my worship of God forever. This part that I am about to tell you, changed my life the most here on earth. I experienced something about God the Father that changed the way I look at life altogether. It has been hard to explain this to others, typically Christians. When you, as a pure spirit being, get to look at the Father, you see Him completely different than you have seen Him before.

The Father's Love Song

Let me attempt to tell each of you reading this now what I am talking about. I pray that the heart of your understanding is open to receive what I have come to know about our Father God.

Before the Throne, after I saw all that I stated in this chapter, I heard another sound that I had a hard time accepting when I got back to earth. It was a sound that I knew brought me life, and life more abundantly. This sound was God the Father singing back to each and every being giving Him praise before the Throne.

He was singing an individual love song to each of His creation. The song was alive and seemed to go inside of the beings it was meant for. What I saw was like what you read in the Song of Solomon in the Bible. Just like in the book Song of Solomon, there is an exchange of love words to each person expressing their love for the other. That is what was going on in heaven. The Father God was expressing His love for each being and they were expressing their love for Him.

I now believe that happens to us here on earth when we express our love to God. I have not tried to copy His song. What really got me was that when He sang the song and it came out of His Spirit, Himself, the song was not touched by any other creation of His. Nothing in heaven stopped it or would think to stop the song from reaching the targeted being.

His Love Song For Us Only

With the songs from the beings to the Father who sits on the Throne, the Crystal-like Sea had its part and the colors had their part. But when it came to God's song, no one had a part but Him, and the being it was meant for. This song was pure love. I understood by seeing this love song come from the Father, the power of love.

I knew that not only was the Father sending a love song to each and every creation of His in heaven, but also on earth. He is sending love to each and every person on the planet. All the time love from God is being sent out to each and every person and nothing can stop this love from reaching us. We can deny His love, reject His love or act like His love is not there, but He keeps sending it to us. I wish people would really get a hold of what I am writing here. I have stated this before, that every time we take a breath of air, He is saying, *"I love you."* If you now take a breath of air, listen to the Father telling you that He loves you.

"For God So Loved The World" became more alive to me in seeing and hearing this love song from the Father to each being there. I came to understand that if for some reason, Jesus did not follow through with His part of redeeming us humans on earth, the Father God was going to find another away to reach us and redeem us. He loves us that much!

I Realized My Home Is Yet To Come

I walked into the sanctuary
Not knowing what to expect
All I knew was
I was tired, bone deep
I sat down in the front pew
Hoping to hear
Hear something
I just needed something

A man came to the podium to speak
He had a kind face
An honest face
So rare
He started talking of a place
It was a place I knew of
But had never been made real
A place called heaven
When he talked
I became entranced
I could see the water
I could see the color
He was describing my childhood memories
The fields I had run
The trees I had climbed
The ocean I had played in
The safety I felt in my parent's home
The love I had felt
The songs they sang over me
Knowing they were watching over me
The completeness, wholeness
I longed for those days again
To feel so carefree
To know you were always loved
To never know fear
But that was not my childhood
That was what was to come
I almost wanted to cry
How did I have memories,
Of a place I had never been?
Why did I feel
Like he just described
my childhood home?
The congregation stands up to go home

But my home wasn't home anymore
I realized
my home is yet to come.
By Teresa Smith

Chapter 17

God's Creation Of Beings

֍

The following is what kind of beings I saw in heaven. There are those who had been humans here on earth and now are among the redeemed in heaven. These beings had been on earth and had made Jesus their Lord and Savior while living on this earth.

Then there are the heavenly creations. They are beings also, but have never known what it is like to be redeemed. As I stated earlier why I call them beings, is that they are BEING everything they were created to be. They are perfect in every way, just as the Father, Jesus and Holy Spirit are perfect. All I saw was perfect beings. They are RIGHT just like everything around them is RIGHT. They are the rightness for God because of what Jesus has done for those who had been human here on earth, and for those heavenly beings who never chose to follow Satan.

All of God's beings were being everything that God had created them to be. They were just shining with the glory of the God of all creation. I was experiencing the creation of God as He created it. I experienced life as He created life. I saw life created.

My Family And Friends Welcome Me

One of the events, that again, blew up one of the boxes that I had believed about heaven, had to do with families. I had believed that you may recognize your family in heaven, but I did not really believe it mattered if you did or not. I just looked at it as we were all in the family of God and that is what counted, and that is true. We are all the family of God.

Now something happened to me that I did not expect to happen when I was in heaven.

Jesus stood to the left of me at about 10 or 11 O'clock. As I said before, Jesus was addressing a half circle of beings, and on the other side of Him to my left, was my family. I saw my Grandmother Mary, Grandfather Lewis, Grandmother Ruth, Grandfather Begron, and many of my parents' brothers and sisters. I also saw friends I knew that had died and others I did not know had died. Also, there were a lot of beings that were related to me, but I had never seen them here on earth during my life time. I understood they were relatives that had died before I died. They went back for generations and generations.

At first, I did not know why they were there, but my Grandmother Mary communicated it to me why they had all come. She stood out in front of all the others who were my family members and friends. She downloaded into me that they came to greet me into heaven. Every family member whom I was connected with because of the DNA inside of me was there; the DNA that God had made me out of.

There were also past friends that showed up. They had all come to greet me into heaven. It was going to be a great family reunion if Jesus had not sent me back, and that was because others here on earth prayed that my body would be healed. To even think about it now, brings me great joy.

My Grandmother Mary

I believe the reason my Grandmother Mary was out in front is because I have always given her credit for praying me into the Kingdom of God. As a child growing up, I can remember going to visit my Grandmother Mary in Houston, Texas. In her house she had a radio on in the kitchen that always had Christian preaching and singing on it. As you went past the kitchen you couldn't help but hear the radio show that was on. I first heard George Foreman preaching on that radio. This was before he came out with his grills.

So I knew she had some kind of connection with God. After I accepted Jesus as Lord and Savior at age 17, I told her. She died before I really could talk to her about being born again. So when I got to heaven it was in my heart to see my Grandmother Mary, if that was possible. I was not really sure as I stated earlier. So the one person out in front was her.

I have come to believe that those of you that long to see a family member, who has gone on to heaven before you, will meet this family member right after you meet Jesus. I believe everyone who has made Jesus their Lord and Savior will meet Him first above all else. Your spirit inside of you (the real you) longs to be with your Lord and Savior.

This event changed how I look at my own family. I did not know what my three brothers, or my dad's relationship to God was. It looked to me as if they did not have a relationship with Jesus. I knew about my mother because she and I would talk about God every time I called her. We would also pray for each other. So I was sure about her relationship with God.

I know that it is up to Jesus and not me to save them, but I wanted to show them the love of God as I had never done before. I just remembered when my older brother and dad were coming through that curtain when I was in the ICU and how I said to myself, "I do not know these people." Because of my belief in Jesus I had pulled away from my family. I did not have the same interests that they had. So I just did not put a lot of effort into keeping a close relationship with them.

Family Matters In Heaven

With that encounter in heaven with my family members I came to know how important families are to God. I remember experiencing the love they had for me. They still love us even when they are in heaven. My family members and friends had pure love for me. They were glad I was there and they desired for me to be with them. This desire was strong. Stronger than the desires we have when praying for our loved ones while we are still living here on earth.

This desire they had for me to be with them is the same desire we have for our loved ones to live with us on earth forever. People here have asked me if they pray for us there. I said, "No, they have a great desire for us to be with them there." Where everything is right, everything is perfect, everything is the way God wants it to be.

I understood that they do not want to come back here to be on earth. They are being everything they were created to be. This is not just my family, but every family member of yours that accepted Jesus as Lord and Savior. They are waiting for you to be with them. They are not there praying for you as I said, they just have a great desire for you to be there with them, just like Jesus. They have a perfect desire for you to be with them. They really do still love you. I came to understand why we grieve when someone dies. We were never meant to be apart. That was not in God's plans for us. We die on this earth because of sin and only because of sin.

Bring Back As Many As You Can!

As I stated earlier, my Grandmother Mary looked at me and downloaded a message for others and me. She told me to bring as many of us back as I can. I understood that she wanted me to bring as many of our family members back with me as I could. I knew that everyone's family members desired the same thing. They want you that know Jesus as Lord and Savior, to bring as many of your relatives and friends as you can, with you to heaven.

I came to understand that this is one of the main reasons Jesus sent me back, is to tell you. Jesus has sent us to our own family first. He wants us to talk to, and to be praying for them. I remember telling a person here on earth that it would be a shame if she was the last person in her family to make it to heaven. It would be a shame. It would be a terrible, terrible shame.

I know that some of you come out of families that you would never think any of them would make it to heaven, but remember that you have come out of that family! I know God is doing everything short of evil to reach them. He has reached you and is reaching you now as you read this testimony. Just as my Grandmother Mary said to me, "Bring back as many of your family members with you to heaven as you can," I believe that all of us should reach as many of our family members as we can. If we that know Jesus as Lord and Savior will reach our own family members, we would reach a lot of people on this planet.

What People Looked Like

My family members in heaven and others who had been human beings here on earth were shining and had pure joy. They shine with the glory of God. This shine looked like a long robe but it was the glory of Jesus coming out of the beings. That is the only reason they are shining. It is Jesus' brightness shining out of them that makes it look like a robe. It moves as if the wind is blowing it all the time, because it is the glory of Jesus and His glory is alive. They had the life of Jesus coming out of them and clothing them in a shining light. This is why there is no darkness. Everything has the

145

glory of God coming out of it. There is no place where darkness can hide. These beings also had a big smile. This was the pure joy that they have.

Are Children There?

They did not age because there is no time in heaven. People ask me all the time if there are children in heaven. I tell them that there is no time in heaven, so there is not any aging in heaven. This does not mean that I did not see what we call children, or young people or old people. There is just no age in heaven. They are all beings and they can show you themselves as they want you to see them. They can show themselves as they were when they were young, old or as a child when they were on earth. So, there are no children in Heaven as we know children here. There is no growing up in heaven because there is no time. I knew that children below the age of accountability will go to heaven. So all aborted children are in heaven, but they are not there as children. They are being everything that God had created them to be. They are beings with pure joy and a big smile.

We Will Still Have Free Will There

Every being had the ability to think in heaven. They still had the right to choose what they did in heaven. They just choose the right thing all the time. They all have the ability to move fast. Like I said earlier, all I had to do was think it, and I was there. They all have the ability to have pure love for others. They had more spiritual gifts than you can ever think of here. The only way a person can come close to understanding what they will be like in heaven is from the Bible. I was a spiritual being that was made in the image of God. I was being what God had made me to be from the beginning of the beginning. I was home and I knew it. You will be home and know it, and you will never leave.

What Will We Be Doing In Heaven?

Since you are there forever, you are fulfilling your purpose in heaven. I had great joy, and the other beings around me had great joy. They were fulfilling their purpose in heaven. I have been asked a number of times what we will do there. When I was there, I saw beings doing so many things to fill in a part of the creation of God. Some of the beings were before the throne of the Father praising Him. I saw them at every area of praise that I wrote about earlier in this book, singing, dancing, flying and more. Some beings were in the half circle before Jesus listening to Him give out orders. They had a part to play in the strategizing commanded by Jesus. I have not found the words to tell of everything I saw other beings doing in heaven, but I knew they all did it with joy. No one was thinking that their purpose was any less than anyone else's purpose. They all knew that their purpose was important in God's Kingdom.

Some of these purposes were to wait on Jesus and the Father. Every creation of God was serving each other. There were no top or bottom. Every creation was equal. I saw every creation of God working with the living water, trees, flowers, mountains, valleys, other planets, and what we would call outer space. I saw beings doing something with suns and stars, helping to move them. I saw beings working with other heavenly beings that we call angels.

Some Of The Bible Saints I Saw

I saw Mary who had brought forth Jesus on earth doing something with the living water there in heaven. What she was doing, I cannot explain to anyone here on earth, because I have not found the words to explain it.

I saw Peter and James in the half circle before Jesus. They had a part in the heavenly army of God. I know they were commanders of some type. I saw them move with each commandment Jesus gave to the unit around them.

I knew that Paul was a part of what goes on with praise and worship here on earth. But again, I do not have the English words to say what I knew he was doing, but it had something to do with dancing and praising the Lord down here on earth. Abraham had a place that seemed so awesome before the Throne of God. He was taking living light and lifting it up to the Throne of God. God would take it within His hands and toss it in the atmosphere. Now, how do I paint this picture for others to understand?

There were more beings doing amazing things of purpose for Jesus and the Father. I just came to understand that we have spiritual gifts that are not added on, but they are us. Our spiritual gifts here on earth are the gifts given to us for the Kingdom of God.

Chapter 18

This Is Not Our Home

2 Corinthians 4:18 (NKJV)
while we do not look at the things which are seen,
but at the things which are not seen. For the things
which are seen are temporary, but the things
which are not seen are eternal.

Everything is right and everyone has the right to be in a place of right. Everything there is alive and everyone has a right to live with God forever. I understood that is why we are here; to tell others of who Jesus is so that they can go and be with God.

2 Corinthians 5:1 (NKJV)
For we know that if our earthly house, this tent, is
destroyed, we have a building from God, a house
not made with hands, eternal in the heavens.

Everything is alive there, and no death exists there. God is pure life, light, and love.

We Are Just Passing Through

When I was there, I knew that I was just passing through down here on earth. It was great to really know that this was not my home. I have always felt that this was not my home, but when I was there, I knew without a doubt that I was just passing through.

Jesus wants me to make sure when I tell my story, that everyone I talk to knows that this is not our home and we who know Jesus as Lord and Savior, are just passing through. Earth is the minority compared to heaven, where the Father God and Jesus are, and the home of the Holy Spirit. It seemed to me that this earth was just a small part of the big picture, a very small part. But we seem to think and act as if this is only it.

This Earth Is Not Our Home

We are ambassadors here, we who know Jesus as Lord and Savior. Most of us agree with that, but do not feel that way here. We act as if this is our home forever, yet Jesus told us that He goes to prepare a place for us. He was not talking about a house as we say many times, but a place in heaven just for us. When I was there, I knew that I was in my place and no one else could take it. It was prepared for me. I also knew that I was not taking anyone else's place. When I talk about the music there, I understood that each being's song had its own place. I knew I was in my place and no one could take it away. Jesus has a place in heaven just for you that know Him as Lord and Savior. It was made just for you and no one else.

This is not our home. This earth is deteriorating. We are in a countdown to the end of the age. The Bible tells us that. I was reading just the other day how the temperature has increased on an average of 30% more since the 1950's. That means the earth is getting hot. We have heard from scientists for sometime that this is happening. We hear about the rain forest and all the trees being cut down, and what that is doing to this earth. Just the other day, I also read how the Coho Salmon in my area are polluted and we should not eat so many of them, especially children and pregnant women because they can cause cancer. Then, they went on to talk about other fish in the Puget Sound here Washington State, and how they were polluted and not to eat so many of them. I could go on about this, but we all are hearing this same information. And yet we are trying to make this our home, knowing it is not. Today's earth is not as good as yesterday's earth and tomorrow's earth is not as good as today's.

My Grandmother Mary wanted me to get this across to other family members here on earth. This was a great desire of her and other beings in heaven. This is a desire of all of God's creation. This is the only desire of our Savior to all of mankind. God Himself, wants us to know this is not our home and we are only passing through. We will outlast every problem we have. We all are going to have to leave this earth someday. We will live on, either in heaven with God, or in hell where everything is wrong, but we are going to have to leave.

The Elderly Lady

I remember after sharing this story in a United Methodist Church in Seattle, Washington, I met an elderly lady who was 91 years old. She had a stroke a few weeks before we came to share and could not talk or move. She was in a wheel chair when I met her. I looked in her eyes and I knew she believed, Oh how she believed! I saw faith in her eyes. I have heard people talk about that kind of faith, but I never saw it like that. When I looked in her eyes, it seemed as if they were saying, "Thank you, thank you and thank you." Then, they seemed to change a little, and it seemed to me she was saying, "Will you come and visit me?" I said to her, "I will come and see you." She then pulled me down to where my ear was close to her mouth and she asked, "When?" The pastor had told me that she could not talk or move. When she had pulled me down and said, "When?", it was the first word she had spoken since having the stroke. That was a glorious time to experience that. I did go see her a few weeks later in a nursing home and she was moving and talking a lot more.

When I died, I knew where to go and no one was telling me where to go. I was like a salmon going home. No one had to tell me. And when I got there, I knew I was supposed to be in my place. And everything was right, I was right where I was supposed to be. I was home. I was home. I WAS HOME!

Chapter 19

Angels

❧

"Angel" is a word often used to describe a supernatural appearance of a heavenly being. (Luke 24:34, Acts 2:3; 7:2,30,35; 9:17; 13:31; 16:9; 26:16).

As I have gone out and told this story, I have had a lot of questions about angels asked to me. Now, I have not focused on angels for one reason. We as humans like to make gods out of God's creations and angels are one of them. Humans like to make gods out of evil spirits, devils and demons. So in writing about what I saw in heaven where the Father and Jesus are, when it comes to angels, understand that angels are one of God's creations and we are not to worship them in any way. They are made for His purpose. They are not to be worshipped. Only God (Father, Son, and Holy Spirit) are to be worshipped. Only God.

We would see more angels, but they do not want to be seen or to be worshipped. I came to really understand this because of what happened to me. Worship and praise was only made for God.

To understand what I am going to write about angels, you must first understand the meaning of the word "angels".

Hebrew Meaning: mal'ak Kalm 1a) messenger, representative 1b) messenger 1c) angel 1d) the theophanic angel
From an unused root meaning to dispatch as a deputy; a messenger; specifically, of God, i.e. an angel (also a prophet, priest or teacher):-ambassador, angel, king, messenger.

Greek Meaning: aggelos aggelov: a messenger, envoy, one who is sent, an angel, a messenger from God.
From aggello (to bring tidings); a messenger; especially an "angel";
by implication, a pastor:-angel, messenger.

The name does not denote their nature, but their office as messengers. In heaven there are no angels, they are looked at as a loving creation of God. They are only an angel when they are being a messenger from God to others.

Now that you have these meanings let us look at these verses to understand that angels come in every size and shape. Some look like humans and some do not.

Revelation 4:6-9 (NKJV)
Before the throne there was a sea of glass, like crystal. And in the midst of the throne, and around the throne, were four living creatures full of eyes in front and in back. The first living creature was like a lion, the second living creature like a calf, the third living creature had a face like a man, and the fourth living creature was like a flying eagle. The four living creatures, each having six wings, were full of eyes around and within. And they do not rest day or night, saying: "Holy, holy, holy, Lord God Almighty, Who was and is and is to come!" Whenever the living creatures give glory and honor and thanks to Him who sits on the throne, who lives forever and ever

Now what I did see, were these creations of God at work. There are a lot of activities here on earth from all the angels working at the command of God. They are part of a massive army fighting for the souls of humans. Every one of them has a purpose and is very happy in completing their purpose. They also have great joy and smile a lot.

The Horse-Like Angels

The first angels that I really did notice were what we call horses. There were so many horses. It was surprising to me. And yet when you read the Bible you see in Revelation where Jesus is coming back on a white horse. There is also a red, a black, and a pale horse mentioned.

Now not every horse looks like what we think horses should look like. Some have the head of a horse and the body of a human. Some have a head of a human and the body of a walking upright horse. Each horse-like being has a purpose. Some were at the Throne, and others were with Jesus when He was addressing the other beings. But they were all moving to the will of God by choice. All the angels still have a choice to serve God.

Some horse beings had wings. Some had wings like a shark fin, and others had two or more wings like birds, bats, and helicopters. Yes, it was different than what I thought it would be. These horses were moving all over the place and moving very fast.

We look at many of the beings as being animals but they are not animals like we have here on earth. In heaven they are just beings made by God.

The Little Angels

There are very little angels that remind me of fairies. They are not fairies, but they are angels or heavenly beings. One person asked me if the little angels have just as much power as the bigger angels do. The smaller angels have just as much power as the bigger angels do because they are working under the authority of God. It is God that gives them power. We think of power as big. It has everything to do with God's love. God's entire Kingdom moves in the power of God's love and this is REAL power. When we understand who really has the power and what that power is, we will overcome a number of things that get in the way of God's love expressed to us.

The Bull-Like Angel

Now another angel that I saw resembles a bull. The bull-like being was big, about seven feet tall. He was shiny just like all the other beings there. The bull-like being had the body of a human with hands, but the feet were like that of a bull's feet. He looked mean to me at first. I saw a ring coming out of his nose and the ring was alive. When I looked in his eyes I saw love. Pure love. He loved all of God's creation that is right. His purpose was to fight for righteousness. In any battle that takes place for righteousness, this being is there, fighting in the spiritual dimension. There was more than one.

The Angels Are Fulfilling God's Purpose

God has lots of angels that do the same for hope, salvation, faith, healing, and much more. You see, our battle is first in the heavenlies, before it is transferred down here on earth.

Ephesians 6:12 (NKJV)
For we do not wrestle against flesh and blood, but against principalities, against powers, against the rulers of the darkness of this age, against spiritual hosts of wickedness in the heavenly places.

All of God's (Father, Son, Holy Spirit) creation is beautiful in His purpose. Purpose combined with God's love makes all of God's creation beautiful. So what do angels look like? Well, like every creation on earth and more. Anything here on earth that is alive could be looked at as an angel in heaven. They are all doing what they are created to do for God in heaven with love. They are messengers of love to us from God.

I know this is hard for us to hear because we look at ourselves as gods here instead of an extension of God's Love to others. The angels of God know this and act in this way. They do all they do within the love of God. In the will of God is beauty, so all you need to know, is that.

Do We Have Guardian Angels?

One of the most asked questions I get is, "Do we have Guardian Angels?" The answer is yes. They do what God has ordered them to do for us. They follow His will. We have more than one. How many does each person have that knows Jesus as Lord and Savior? How many we have is based on if you are fulfilling your purpose here on earth. They are all doing what they are created to do for God in heaven with love. There are no weaker angels, as I stated earlier. It all has to do with God's purpose for them.

This war that is going on is bigger than most of us want to believe. Everyone trusting our Father for a breakthrough has more going on around in the spiritual dimension than they will know. For everyone that has come to know Jesus as Lord and Savior, there was a great battle that took place in the spiritual dimension for your soul. Since the fall of Lucifer, many angels have taken their place in the battle. Again, they are messengers of love to us from God.

What Do Angels Look Like?

Maybe one out of four angels looked human. There are angels that look like human men and women, but their reputation of being male and female does not affect their purpose. Angels are genderless; they only look like male or female. There are angels that look like light, fire, water, air, clouds, wind, trees, and flowers. I could go on, but really understand this one thing; they are all beautiful because they are doing God's will. In the will of God is beauty. Again, remember that is all you need know to understand that.

So just know that there are more angels that stayed with God (Father, Son, Holy Spirit) than went with Satan. Some day I will teach on this area about angels more, when I think it will not lead to more angel worship. I end this chapter with this - we are only to worship God (Father, Son, Holy Spirit), and not angels.

Our Guardian Angels

When you're asleep and all alone,
your guardian angels are protecting you.
Our angels are there and will always be,
so don't be afraid and just go to sleep.
By Alexandra Kenyon – age 12

Chapter 20

Eight Things I Was Told About The End Of The Age

꧁꧂

When I was in heaven with Jesus and the Father, Jesus downloaded these eight things to signal the end of the age. They were not given to me to put in a certain order. Some are happening right now, others are beginning to happen, and others are coming. The one I like a lot, talks about praying a lot and eyes opening. We need to be in more prayer, for us to see what God sees.

THESE EIGHT THINGS WILL TAKE PLACE TO SIGNAL THE END OF THE AGE!
(They are not in any order.)

EVERY NATION IS HERE FOR THE PURPOSE OF GOD!

KINGS AND QUEENS, OR WHAT YOU CALL PRESIDENTS AND PRIME MINISTERS, ARE ALL PUT IN POWER FOR THE PURPOSE OF GOD!

MORE, EVERYDAY, SONS AND DAUGHTERS OF GOD WILL BE PLACED IN RULERSHIP OF NATIONS FOR THE PURPOSE OF GOD!

RAISING PEOPLE FROM THE DEAD WILL BE COMMON IN THE LAST DAYS OF THE AGE!

GOD IS NOT WORKING THROUGH ONE PERSON, BUT THROUGH HIS SONS AND DAUGHTERS IN THE PRESENT AGE. STOP PEOPLE FROM CHASING MEN AND HAVE THEM FOLLOW GOD!

THE GOOD NEWS OF GOD IS NOT FOR SALE AND HE IS GOING TO STOP THE SELLING OF IT BY HAVING MORE PEOPLE GIVE WHAT THEY KNOW AWAY. FREELY IT HAS BEEN GIVEN AND FREELY THEY MUST GIVE!

THAT WHICH IS EVIL WILL LOOK GOOD, EVEN TO THE SONS AND DAUGHTERS OF GOD. THE SONS AND DAUGHTERS OF GOD WILL GROW IN PRAYER IN THAT TIME, AND NEW EYES WILL OPEN - SPIRITUAL EYES. THEY WILL SEE FROM THE HEART!

VISUAL DECEPTION WILL INCREASE IN ALL AREAS OF THE WORLD!

Chapter 21

What Was I In Heaven?

W hat was it like to be in heaven as a being? You are being who God truly made you to be. You lack nothing.

There, you are a part of everything and everything is a part of you. You experience everything there, all at once. All at one time, your current spiritual gifts explode and keep the intensities. It is like jumping into cold water and all of your senses being activated at the same time, but in a good way. Imagine smelling, tasting, seeing, feeling, and hearing the water all at the same time. That is how it is in heaven when it comes to your spiritual gifts.

Our Spiritual Gifts And Abilities

There are added spiritual gifts to the ones you have here on earth. You really have more spiritual gifts than you have here on earth. No drug here on earth can compare with what you will experience there. There, everything is made to be a part of you. When you see something, you experience it with no imperfection.

We do not always use our spiritual gifts here in a consistent way. We have the ability to use them all the time, but in the fight with our carnal self, we come up short. We just do not use them as often as we should, here on earth. But there, we have more spiritual gifts than here. There are more new spiritual gifts that come alive when you are in heaven. I just do not have anything here on earth to compare with these other spiritual gifts. There are spiritual gifts that you have never experienced here on earth.

How I Traveled In Heaven

Just like we have new spiritual gifts, we have new abilities to do things we cannot do in this body. Since coming back, I have come to understand more about my body and what it can and cannot do. In heaven, my spirit has no limits; not like my body here on earth. You move fast. When I left this body, I was at Jesus' feet faster than a person can blink. When I wanted to move, I just thought of being somewhere else and I was there.

I could pass through anything and everything, not that you did because of respect for other beings. I would always ask for permission. When you enter a room you could go through what we call walls. But again remember, everything is alive, even the buildings. The buildings have doors and gates, but I did not have to use them. Now, I would out of respect for the buildings, because they were alive. Everything is alive, so I would ask. I was at the top of mountains, bottom of seas or water, in trees, under bushes, on dirt or ground, walking through grass and flowers. I did all of this just by thinking about it. I would fly, or what we would call flying. It was more like just being in the atmosphere, the goldest white atmosphere. What an atmosphere! Yes, the atmosphere is alive.

What more can I write? It is hard to explain to others what "everything is right" feels like. It is not a feeling but an experience. It is hard for others to understand with their mind what it is like where the Father and Jesus are. That is something you will only understand when you come to know who you really are - a created spirit of God. Because we are spirit, soul, and body, we have to let our spirit become alive in God's Kingdom. We have the ability to choose who we serve; whether it is God or ourselves.

What did I look like? I was shining because of the Father and Jesus. They shined out of me.

Chapter 22

Who Am I Now After Heaven?

❧

When I was in the hospital knowing that I had been to heaven and back, I did not want to misuse this gift that I had experienced. I prayed to God and asked Him to help me not be tempted to make a lot of money off of this experience. Even if I had great riches here on earth, what would they be compared to what I have in heaven? Not a thing. When you have Jesus, you have everything you need.

So the Father God and I came up with two things for me to follow to stay away from pride.

One, is to have my wife speak before me when she is with me, to give her as much time as she needs to tell her side of the story. I have been in places where they have given us an hour to speak and she has taken 45 minutes to tell her side of the story. That left me with only 15 minutes. Most of the time people have asked me to keep going or have asked us back. But my wife, when she speaks, can take as much time as she wants to tell what she knows.

I have always felt like I have a special message for each and every person I have come back to talk to. Numbers are not a big thing to me. God knows who He sent me back to. I just have to go and tell them. I have presented to thousands of people at a time, or just one person at a time. I have had the honor to speak just to one family, from great grandparents to great, great grandchildren all in the same family. Whoever they are does not matter to me as long as I speak to who God wants me to speak to. All I have to do is do what He wants me to do.

I Only Talk About What People Ask Me

The other area that God and I came up with to keep me from pride is that I would not talk about anything that I have not been asked a question about. All that I have written in this book is based on questions that people have asked me about the experience. I would have question and answer sessions so that people would ask me as many questions as possible. I have been in some question and answer meetings that lasted up to six hours. There are still many questions that have not been asked.

Before going to heaven and coming back, I would stay away from anything that had to do with people asking me questions about the Bible. I knew why I believed in what I believed, but I did not want to answer questions on things I did not know about or even things I did know about. I did not want to get into any arguments over anything when it came to the Bible.

The other reason I did not like to answer questions is because I did not want others to know that I did not know something (being a minister). But now, I am ready to take on any question given me. If I do not know, that is OK. I say to people many times that I only need to know what God wants me to know. Most people I say that to, do not understand what I am saying. But when I was in heaven, there was no wasting anything. So I try not to use my thinking on things that are not important.

Four Main Areas Of Questions

First are from children. Their most asked question is, "Is it going to be fun in heaven?" They ask some of the best questions. Children ask the most questions that are "out of the box". Much of what I tell people come from their questions. They just seem to have this way of thinking that they know they are going to heaven; they just want to know how much fun they are going to have.

Second, are from teenagers. Their questions are questions to get more information to deal with their belief system. They want to know more about this God. Is He really real? They also have a way of asking questions "outside of the box".

Third, are from some adults. Their questions are questions to support their beliefs. They want to find out if God fits in the box they've created for Him. Sometimes I support what someone had believed before. Sometimes I expand on what someone had believed about God. And sometimes I give them information that just blows up the box they built for God. I tell them many times that He did not fit in the box that I had created for Him. As you have read, many of these boxes were blown up that I had put God in.

Fourth, are from the elderly. Their questions are questions along the same lines as children ask. They are coming to the reality that they are close to going home, and just want to know how it is going to be.

There are adults that ask questions like a child, teenager, or elderly too.

My Number One Job

I ask everyone who reads this to understand that I have a job to do down here on earth, and until it is done I cannot go back home. What is that job? To bring back as many people with me as I can, no different than anyone else who has accepted Jesus as their Lord and Savior.

When I was in heaven I had pure joy. I know that everyone who comes before Jesus as a son of God will have pure joy. Anyone who Jesus can see Himself in, that person will have pure joy. I also know that those that come before Jesus that do not know Him as Lord and Savior will experience pure terror. The greatest pain a person who has not accepted Jesus as Lord and Savior will experience, is not being with Jesus forever, not being with the Creator, not having Jesus within them.

I know that I am not a part of this world as I felt before. Even when I knew I was going to be with God someday, I still felt like this was home for now. Now after my experience, I do not feel like this is my home at all. My home is with God, my Father. I even call the time that I take to pray, going home. For me, praying is like going home for a time. I sometimes just want to pray all day, for I feel at home in praying. Even to write it down for you to read, brings me to the point of wanting to stop and pray. I know He hears our prayers. Yes, we that know Jesus as Lord and Savior, He hears our prayers from our heart, not from our head.

It's Taken Some Time To Re-Adjust

There are times when I feel very out of place here on earth. I can retreat inward for long periods of time. I feel as if I never left there. I will be glad when all this mess on earth is over and every part of God's creation is right.

It seems to me that I am in between two dimensions, the real and the not-real. For most people, the earth is the real dimension and heaven is not. For me, it is the other way around. I see this world falling apart every day. I know that today is better than tomorrow and yesterday was better than today. I do not mean in my spirit and God's kingdom, I am actually talking about the physical world we live on. The ground, trees, plants, water, and everything we can see, hear, and touch. It is falling apart because of the curse that was brought on us by Adam, man. I see it falling apart everyday. This is good and bad. In me, I cry to have more saved, and at the same time I feel and see how short the time is that we have. So what is the real dimension?

I think a lot slower now when answering others. I do not like to waste words. What I mean by this is, we say a lot of things that are just the answer we are used to giving. Here is an example: "How are you doing?" Most people say, "Good" or "OK", or something that we have been programmed to answer with. Now, I have to make sure that I am the words I say, because there, in heaven, you waste no words. Communication was all right, so you did not say a lot, but what you did say was truth.

Now again, you did not communicate with words out loud that much. You could if you wanted to, but mostly every being just gave you what they were thinking. I say like a computer downloading. Sometimes I ask my wife or son something in my head and believed I said it out loud. They have now helped me to remember to talk out loud. Sometimes I have to remind myself to talk out loud too. I do not have the need to pray out loud so others can hear me. I know My Father hears me loud and clear whether I say it out loud or not. It must come from my heart. I know He hears me and will answer my prayer.

Praying for the sick, that have Jesus as their Lord and Savior, was hard. I knew that if they died they would go to heaven to be with my Father, their Father. But, God let me know, until their purpose is done on earth I am to always pray for healing. And the other thing is, God is the only one who knows when a child of God's time is up.

It is hard for me to receive any praise for what I do or say now. When I was with the Father and Jesus in heaven, only the Father and Jesus received praise.

I now know this more than I had before. That, "relation-ship" is the only thing that will last. We can take a relationship we have with another child of God with us to heaven. When people come to know Jesus as Lord and Savior through how I am serving my Father, I will have a relationship with them forever. And it will be all right. Yes!

Chapter 23

Last Comments

❦

Over the past 33 years I have worked with people in the social field, mostly with teenagers and their families. I worked in King County Superior Court employed as a Juvenile Drug Court/Chemical Dependency Disposition Alternative Program Manager.

I have also worked as a Program/Project Manager for King County's Mental Health, Chemical Abuse and Dependency Service Division. I was employed in the U.S. Air Force active duty for six years and the Air Force Reserve for another 14 years, with 18 of those years as a Chemical Dependency Counselor and Human Relations and Equal Opportunity Counselor. In the past, I have been a Director for an inpatient treatment/transitional-housing program, a Substance Abuse Prevention Coordinator for King County, and a Chemical Dependency Coordinator for two outpatient youth treatment programs. I have helped train over 400 parents in parenting skills and given over 1000 trainings and presentations dealing with subjects addressing human service issues. I have coordinated prevention, treatment, family conferences, and have been on television and radio discussing subjects concerning human services issues. I helped develop a number of model programs that have been funded by the U.S. government, King County and private industries. I have been on many committees representing Washington State, King County, and many cities.

About two years ago I left this work to tell this story to as many people as possible. I have done it across the United States and in other countries. But what is on my heart, is to reach the young people all around the world. In my heart are many young people who have not really had an encounter with the all-powerful God.

In the coming years I am praying that I can make this heavenly experience a reality to the youth of this world. I hope to do this through a number of ways: Comics, Videos, Video/Board Games, clothing, music, and many more books. Somehow, we must reach that generation that we believe are lost.

I do not want Jesus to come back soon, because there are still so many to tell about Him. I was where He is and He truly wants everyone there. I heard the sounds from hell. If you heard them, you truly would not even want any of your enemies to go there. That is not the will of God.

So, in these last days I am on this earth, I want to reach those kids. Pray that I do and can.

I want to use the resource from this book to reach those kids, support this ministry and support Restoring Hope International Ministries in Peru, South America.

The Restoring Hope International Ministries supports many in Peru. Some of the resources from this book would target the girls' home named Torre Fuerte (Strong Tower) in Arequipa. This home gives shelter and around the clock care to 48 girls ranging from 3-20 years of age. These girls come from juvenile court institutions (what we would call foster care) and even sometimes they are left by parents and grand-parents who are unable to care for them. For more information about Restoring Hope International Ministries go to www.rhintl.org.

Again, we must in these last days, reach as many as we can in our own countries and around the world. We must reach as many as we can before they go to hell and not heaven.

What Are You Going To Do With This Information?

I have done my best to share my experience in this book. I hope this has helped you to really choose who you want to serve in your last days here on earth. I want you to experience all that I did and more. Yes, there is a lot more I did not say, or even experience myself. You see, what we call heaven, is ever-expanding. God is still creating. Nothing dies there. Yes, there is a lot more waiting for you there. I want you to see all of God's living creation.

Right now, make God (Father, Son, and Holy Spirit) the Savior of your soul and spirit, which is the real you. Ask God to become your Lord of your life. Do it in your own words. Or say these: *"Jesus, I ask you to forgive me of all I have done wrong. Those actions I remember and those I do not remember. I want you to be my Savior and Lord now. Thank you for making a way so that I can live with you forever and ever. I ask this in my Savior Jesus' name. Amen."*

For some of you that this does not fix, it's because you said it before. Well now, make a new commitment to him. Ask Him to forgive you for not following through before and to help you follow through this time. Say it in your own words. Say it from your heart.

Now you will know what it is like to say, "You Did This For Me, Thank You, Thank You, Thank You!"

CHAPTER NOTES

꧁꧂

I have listed the scripture references by whole passages in hopes that you would study them in their entire settings to fully understand these verses. You will find that some key scriptures relating to my testimony will be fully printed out or shortened within parenthesis.

Chapter 1 Notes
"No, It Is Not Your Time"

Subtitle: None

Line: *What I do remember, is the first time I was before Jesus He said, "No, It is not your time. Go back."*
Luke 12: 16-21 20 But God said to him, 'Fool! This night your soul will be required of you; then whose will those things be which you have provided?'
Eccl. 9:12, Job 22:15 –16 (verse 16)

Line: *At the edge of heaven is thick darkness - a blackness like you have never experienced here on earth.*
Rev 16:10-11 10 Then the fifth angel poured out his bowl on the throne of the beast, and his kingdom became full of darkness; and they gnawed their tongues because of the pain.
Ex 10:21-23 (verse 22), Mat 8:12, Mat 22:13, Mat 25:30

Line: *This second time I reached the edge of heaven, I heard the cries of those who were in hell.*
Rev 20:13 ...and Death and Hades (Hell) delivered up the dead who were in them.
Job 26:6, Luke 8:26-31 (verse 31)

Subtitle: A Simple Operation

Line: *I know EVERYTHING IS RIGHT, where Jesus is, and THERE IS NOTHING WRONG!*
Ps 119:142 Your righteousness is an everlasting righteousness, Luke 12:32-34 (verse 33), John 8:31-36 (verses 32,36), 2Cor 5:20-21 (verse 21), Phil 3:8-11 (verse 9)

Line: *Some say it is peaceful, **but it far exceeds past peace** because there is nothing to be peaceful from.*
Phil 4:6-9 7 and the peace of God, which surpasses all understanding, will guard your hearts and minds through Christ

Jesus. 9 The things which you learned and received and heard and saw in me, these do, and the God of peace will be with you.
John 14:25-28 (verse 27), Eph 2:14-18 (verses 14,17)

Line: *Some say it is peaceful, but it far exceeds past peace because **there is nothing to be peaceful from.***
Rev 21:22-27 27 But there shall by no means enter it anything that defiles, or causes an abomination or a lie, but only those who are written in the Lamb's Book of Life.

Line: *When I first arrived in heaven and knelt before Jesus, all I could do was say, "YOU DID THIS FOR ME?!! THANK YOU, THANK YOU, THANK YOU, THANK YOU, THANK YOU, and THANK YOU!!"*
Ps 79:13 ...Will give You thanks forever; We will show forth Your praise to all generations.
Ps 34:1-3, Ps 63:2-6 (verses 3-5), Ps 118:19-21 (verses 19,21)

Chapter 2 Notes
I Am Just a Man

Subtitle: None

Line: *I must let everyone know I was sent back to do the same thing that all of us that accept Jesus into our lives as Lord and Savior are supposed to do.*

Mat 28:16-20 19 Go therefore and make disciples of all the nations, baptizing them in the name of the Father and of the Son and of the Holy Spirit, 20 teaching them to observe all things that I have commanded you; and lo, I am with you always, even to the end of the age." Amen.

Mark 16:14-18 (verses 15-18), Luke 24:46-53 (verses 47-48), Acts 1:7-8 (verse 8)

Subtitle: What Really Matters Is That You Are There!

Line: *What will matter, is that you are there!*

Heb 11:15-16 (verse 16) But now they desire a better, that is, a heavenly country. Therefore God is not ashamed to be called their God, for He has prepared a city for them.

John 14:1-6 (verse 6), 2Cor 4:14

Line: *I do not have to perform to get in heaven, and you do not have to perform either.*

Gal 1:10 For if I still pleased men, I would not be a bondservant of Christ.

John 9:4

Line: *There are many people in heaven whom I did not think would make it but did, and many whom I believed would make it but did not. Jesus knows the heart of a person.*

Mat 7:21-23 21 "Not everyone who says to Me, 'Lord, Lord,' shall enter the kingdom of heaven, but he who does the will of My Father in heaven. 23 And then I will declare to

them, 'I never knew you; depart from Me, you who practice lawlessness!'
Mat 22:11-13 (verse 13), Rom 11:19-22 (verses 20-21)

Line: *All I can say is He looked at me and saw Himself in me and I was accepted into heaven.*
Gal 2:17-20 20 I have been crucified with Christ; it is no longer I who live, but Christ lives in me; and the life which I now live in the flesh I live by faith in the Son of God, who loved me and gave Himself for me.
Eph 3:14-19 (verses 16-17), Col 1:27-29 (verse 27)

Chapter 3 Notes
Everything Is Right "You Did This For Me?!!"

Subtitle: Thank You, Thank You, Thank You....
Line: *I repeat that I know everything is RIGHT where Jesus is and there is nothing wrong.*
John 8:31-36 32 And you shall know the truth, and the truth shall make you free." 36 Therefore if the Son makes you free, you shall be free indeed.
Luke 12:32-34 (verse 33), Rev 21:6-7 (verse 7)

Line: *Some say it is peaceful, but it far exceeds past peace because there is nothing to be peaceful from.*
Rev 21:22-27 27 But there shall by no means enter it anything that defiles, or causes an abomination or a lie, but only those who are written in the Lamb's Book of Life.

Line: *When I first got there before Jesus, all I could do was say, "YOU DID THIS FOR ME?!!, THANK YOU, THANK YOU, THANK YOU, THANK YOU, THANK YOU, THANK YOU!"*
Ps 138:1-5 1 I will praise You with my whole heart; Before the gods I will sing praises to You. 2 I will worship toward Your holy temple, And praise Your name For Your loving-kindness and Your truth; For You have magnified Your word above all Your name. 4 All the kings of the earth shall praise You, O LORD, When they hear the words of Your mouth. 5 Yes, they shall sing of the ways of the LORD, For great is the glory of the LORD.
Ps 34:1-3, Ps 63:2-5 (verses 3-5), Ps 79:13, Ps 118:19-21 (verse 19)

Line: *When I first got there, all I wanted to do or could do was praise Jesus.*

Ps 103:1-5 1 Bless the LORD, O my soul; And all that is within me, bless His holy name! 2 Bless the LORD, O my soul, And forget not all His benefits:
Ps 118:15-18 (verse 17), Luke 19:37-40 (verses 37-38)

Line: *No one had to tell me. I just knew what to do. I know we praise Jesus and Father God, no one else.*
John 4:23-24 23 But the hour is coming, and now is, when the true worshipers will worship the Father in spirit and truth; for the Father is seeking such to worship Him. 24 God is Spirit, and those who worship Him must worship in spirit and truth.
Mat 21:15-16 (verse 16), Phil 3:17-21 (verses 20-21)

Line: *The only ones who receive praise are the Father and Jesus in heaven, they are THE ONLY ONES.*
1 Cor 1:27-31 29 that no flesh should glory in His presence. 31 that, as it is written, "He who glories, let him glory in the LORD.
Isa 2:11-12 (verse 11), Rev 21:22-27 (verses 22-23)

Subtitle: Praising Him Was All I Needed
Line: *Everything within me praised Him. Everything I was made of cried out in praise to Jesus.*
Ps 103:1-5 1 Bless the LORD, O my soul; And all that is within me, bless His holy name! 2 Bless the LORD, O my soul, And forget not all His benefits
Ps 118:15-18 (verse 17), Luke 19:37-40 (verses 37-38)

Line: *Not my body (it stayed here on earth), but my spirit and soul - the real me.*
1 Cor 15:50-54 50 Now this I say, brethren, that flesh and blood cannot inherit the kingdom of God; nor does corruption inherit incorruption. 53 For this corruptible must put on incorruption, and this mortal must put on immortality.

54 So when this corruptible has put on incorruption, and this mortal has put on immortality, then shall be brought to pass the saying that is written: "Death is swallowed up in victory."
2 Cor 5:1-10 (verses 1-2,4,6,8), Ps 103:14-17 (verse 14)

Line: *Not my body (it stayed here on earth), but my spirit and soul - the real me.*
John 4:21-24 23 But the hour is coming, and now is, when the true worshipers will worship the Father in spirit and truth; for the Father is seeking such to worship Him. 24 God is Spirit, and those who worship Him must worship in spirit and truth.
Ps 119:171-175 (verse 175), Ps 94:16-19 (verse 17)

Line: *During the praising it seem like I was turning into God's LOVE.*
1 John 4:16-17 16 And we have known and believed the love that God has for us. God is love, and he who abides in love abides in God, and God in him 17 Love has been perfected among us in this: that we may have boldness in the day of judgment; because as He is, so are we in this world.
1 Cor 13:4-8, Eph 5:1-2 (verse 2)

Line: *I had pure JOY. It seems to me that you live off the praising.*
Luke 10:17-20 17 Then the seventy returned with joy, saying, "Lord, even the demons are subject to us in Your name." 20 Nevertheless do not rejoice in this, that the spirits are subject to you, but rather rejoice because your names are written in heaven."
Ps. 4:6-8 (verse 7), Eccl 2:24-26 (verse 26), Isa 12:2-3 (verse 3), Rom 15:13

Line: *You did not need any food. Praising Him seemed to be all you needed.*
John 4:31-34 34 Jesus said to them, "My food is to do the will of Him who sent Me, and to finish His work.
Lam 3:20-26 (verses 22-23)

Line: *Not what I did, but what He did when I accepted Him as my Lord and Savior.*
2 Tim 1:8-10 9 who has saved us and called us with a holy calling, not according to our works, but according to His own purpose and grace which was given to us in Christ Jesus before time began,
Rom 15:17-19 (verse 18), Titus 3:3-9 (verses 5,7-8)

Subtitle: I Saw Jesus On The Cross
Line: *I knew what He did on the cross was for me.*
Rom 10:9-13 13 For "whoever calls on the name of the LORD shall be saved."
Eph 1:3-14 (verse 6), Tit 2:11-12 (verse 11)

Line: *I knew that, I knew.*
1 Cor 13:12-13 12 For now we see in a mirror, dimly, but then face to face. Now I know in part, but then I shall know just as I also am known.
Heb 12:22-24

Line: *The only reason I was there is because of what He had done for me, and I knew it. I knew I was complete or perfect because of what He had done.*
John 3:13-18 14 And as Moses lifted up the serpent in the wilderness, even so must the Son of Man be lifted up, 15 that whoever believes in Him should not perish but have eternal life. 16 For God so loved the world that He gave His only begotten Son, that whoever believes in Him should not perish but have everlasting life. 17 For God did not send His Son into the world

to condemn the world, but that the world through Him might be saved. 18 "He who believes in Him is not condemned; but he who does not believe is condemned already, because he has not believed in the name of the only begotten Son of God.
Is 53:4-5, John 1:29-31 (verse 29)

Line: *The only reason I was there is because of what He had done for me, and I knew it. I knew I was complete or perfect because of what He had done.*
2 Cor 5:16-21 17 Therefore, if anyone is in Christ, he is a new creation; old things have passed away; behold, all things have become new. 19 that is, that God was in Christ reconciling the world to Himself, not imputing their trespasses to them, and has committed to us the word of reconciliation. 21 For He made Him who knew no sin to be sin for us, that we might become the righteousness of God in Him.
Rom 6:1-4 (verse 4), Col 4:12

Line: *I knew He saw Himself in me and I was allowed into Heaven.*
1 John 5:9-12 11 And this is the testimony: that God has given us eternal life, and this life is in His Son. 12 He who has the Son has life; he who does not have the Son of God does not have life.
Luke 12:8-9 (verse 8), 1 John 4:13-16 (verses 13,16)

Line: *It was all of His works. Even the good works I did was Him working through me.*
Col 3:14-24 17 And whatever you do in word or deed, do all in the name of the Lord Jesus, giving thanks to God the Father through Him. 23 And whatever you do, do it heartily, as to the Lord and not to men, 24 knowing that from the Lord you will receive the reward of the inheritance; for you serve the Lord Christ.
Ps. 44:1-3 (verse 3), Phil 2:13-14 (verse 13)

Subtitle: My Place, My Space

Line: *I knew it was for others also, but it just seemed as if it had been made for only me.*

John 14:1-4 2 In My Father's house are many mansions (Literally dwellings place); if it were not so, I would have told you. I go to prepare a place for you.

Line: *I knew I was in my place. No one could take my place.*

Mar 10:37-40 40 but to sit on My right hand and on My left is not Mine to give, but it is for those for whom it is prepared."

John 14:1-2 (verse 2)

Subtitle: I Had No Memory Of Sin

Line: *Another reason I said "you did this for me", is because it was like I had never sinned in my whole life.*

Eph 1:3-6 4 just as He chose us in Him before the foundation of the world, that we should be holy and without blame before Him in love,

2 Cor 5:17-19 (verse 19), Heb 10:11-18 (verse 14)

Line: *I knew I had been set free from true death (sin), and it could not keep me from Jesus and the Father.*

Rom. 6:4-11 4 Therefore we were buried with Him through baptism into death, that just as Christ was raised from the dead by the glory of the Father, even so we also should walk in newness of life. 8 Now if we died with Christ, we believe that we shall also live with Him, 9 knowing that Christ, having been raised from the dead, dies no more. Death no longer has dominion over Him.

1 Cor 6:9-11 (verse 11), 2 Cor 5:17-19 (verse 18)

Line: *I knew I had been set free from true death (sin), and **it could not keep me from Jesus and the Father***

Rom 8: 35-39 35 Who shall separate us from the love of Christ? Shall tribulation, or distress, or persecution, or famine, or nakedness, or peril, or sword? 38 For I am persuaded that neither death nor life, nor angels nor principalities nor powers, nor things present nor things to come, 39 nor height nor depth, nor any other created thing, shall be able to separate us from the love of God which is in Christ Jesus our Lord.
Rev 20:12-15 (verses 14-15), Rev 21:6-8

Line: *I knew I had been set free from **true death** (sin), and it could not keep me from Jesus and the Father.*
Rev 1:17-18 18 I am He who lives, and was dead, and behold, I am alive forevermore. Amen. And I have the keys of Hades and of Death.
Rom 5:8-9 (verse 9), Rom 5:18-21 (verses 18-19)

Line: *I had no remembrance of sinning at all.*
2 Cor 5:17-19 19 that is, that God was in Christ reconciling the world to Himself, not imputing their trespasses to them, and has committed to us the word of reconciliation.
Jer 31:32-34 (verse 34), Eph 1:3-6

Line: *And I knew Jesus could not have reminded me, for I was forgiven and He did not remember any of my sins.*
1 John 1:5-10 9 If we confess our sins, He is faithful and just to forgive us our sins and to cleanse us from all unrighteousness.
Isa 43:25-26 (verse 25), Micah 7:18-19

Line: *Again I knew that I knew, that I knew, and I know.*
Heb 12:22-24 22 But you have come to Mount Zion and to the city of the living God, the heavenly Jerusalem, to an innumerable company of angels, 23 to the general assembly and church of the firstborn who are registered in heaven, to God

the Judge of all, to the spirits of just men made perfect, 24 to Jesus the Mediator of the new covenant, and to the blood of sprinkling that speaks better things than that of Abel.
1 Cor 13:12-13 (verse 12)

Line: *I knew I could never be separated from my Father and Jesus.*
Rom 5:18-21 18 Therefore, as through one man's offense judgment came to all men, resulting in condemnation, even so through one Man's righteous act the free gift came to all men, resulting in justification of life. 19 For as by one man's disobedience many were made sinners, so also by one Man's obedience many will be made righteous.
Rom 5:8-9 (verse 9)

Line: *I came to understand true death is being separated from God.*
Rev 20:12-15 14 Then Death and Hades were cast into the lake of fire. This is the second death. 15 And anyone not found written in the Book of Life was cast into the lake of fire.
Rom 8:35-39 (verses 35,38-39), Eph 1:15-23 (verses 22-23)

Line: *I came to realize that no one could hurt me.*
Rev 21:22-27 24 And the nations of those who are saved shall walk in its light, and the kings of the earth bring their glory and honor into it. 25 Its gates shall not be shut at all by day (there shall be no night there). 26 And they shall bring the glory and the honor of the nations into it.
Ps 118:6-7 (verse 6)

Chapter 5 Notes
I Have Seen Jesus

Subtitle: Jesus Is Bright

Line: *Jesus is bright.*
Rev 1:12-16 16 He had in His right hand seven stars, out of His mouth went a sharp two-edged sword, and His countenance (expression, face) was like the sun shining in its strength.
Mat 17:1-3 (verses 2-3), Acts 9:1-5 (verse 3)

Line: *He was brighter than our sun on a hot sunny noonday and yet you can look at Him.*
Rev 21:22-24 23 The city had no need of the sun or of the moon to shine in it, for the glory of God illuminated it. The Lamb is its light.
Acts 26:12-15 (verse 13), Rev 1:12-16 (verse 16), Rev 22:3-5 (verse 5)

Line: *He was brighter than our sun on a hot sunny noonday and yet you can look at Him.*
John 12:34-36 35 Then Jesus said to them, "A little while longer the light is with you. Walk while you have the light, lest darkness overtake you; he who walks in darkness does not know where he is going. 36 While you have the light, believe in the light, that you may become sons of light." These things Jesus spoke, and departed, and was hidden from them.
Heb 1:1-4 (verse 3), 1 John 1:6-7 (verse 7)

Line: *But those who were RIGHT with Him, could look at Him and have perfect joy.*
1 John 2:28-29 28 And now, little children, abide in Him, that when He appears, we may have confidence and not be ashamed before Him at His coming. 29 If you know that

He is righteous, you know that everyone who practices righteousness is born of Him.
1 John 3:6-7

Line: *But those who were RIGHT with Him, could look at Him and have perfect joy.*
Eccl 2:24-25 25 For God gives wisdom and knowledge and joy to a man who is good in His sight; but to the sinner He gives the work of gathering and collecting, that he may give to him who is good before God. This also is vanity and grasping for the wind.
Rom 15:13, Jude 1:24-25 (verse 24)

Line: *But I knew that if you were not RIGHT with Him, then terror was what you would experience.*
Ps 94:20-23 23 He has brought on them their own iniquity, And shall cut them off in their own wickedness; The LORD our God shall cut them off.
Pr 11:5-9, Pr 11:20-23 (verses 20-21,23)

Line: *You had to look at Him with a pure heart.*
Mat 5:6-9 8 Blessed are the pure in heart, For they shall see God.
1 John 5:9-13 (verses 10 & 12)

Subtitle: His Feet
Line: *They are just like John from the Bible said in Revelations 1:15.*
Rev 1:12-16 15 His feet were like fine brass, as if refined in a furnace, and His voice as the sound of many waters;
Rev 2:18-19 (verse 18)

Line: *He still has the wounds from where the nails pierced his feet.*

Luke 24:38-43 39 Behold My hands and My feet, that it is I Myself. Handle Me and see, for a spirit does not have flesh and bones as you see I have." 40 When He had said this, He showed them His hands and His feet.

Line: *It was not only that He loved me, but that it was like I was the only one He loved in all of His creation.*
Isa. 49:14-16 15 "Can a woman forget her nursing child, And not have compassion on the son of her womb? Surely they may forget, Yet I will not forget you.

Subtitle: His Hands
Line: *Yes, you can see the nail piercings that took place in His hands.*
Luke 24:38-43 39 Behold My hands and My feet, that it is I Myself. Handle Me and see, for a spirit does not have flesh and bones as you see I have." 40 When He had said this, He showed them His hands and His feet.
John 20:24-27 (verses 26-27)

Subtitle: His Body
Line: *Just like the Bible says in 1 John 4:7, God is love*
1 John 4:12-16 16 And we have known and believed the love that God has for us. God is love, and he who abides in love abides in God, and God in him.
Lam 3:20-24 (verses 22-23)
Rom 8:35-39 (verses 35,39)

Line: *I saw what it cost for me to be there, and have a relationship with God Almighty. I did not know before this happened, how much it cost in pain to his physical body, for us to have a relationship with God.*
Isa 52:13-15 14 Just as many were astonished at you, So His visage was marred more than any man, And His form more than the sons of men;

Read Isa. 52:14-15 from the NET BIBLE at bible.org Isa 53:1-2 (verse 2), Isa 53:3-6 (verse 5), Mat. 27:24-50 (26-30), Read Mat 27:24-31 notes from the NET BIBLE at bible.org, Mark 14:41-50 (verses 41,44-45,50), Mark 15:11-15 (verse 15), Read Mark 15:16-20 notes from the NET BIBLE at bible.org, Luke 23:22-25 (verses 23,25)

Line: *You get to see Him as He is, but it is from your heart.*
1 John 3:1-2 2 Beloved, now we are children of God; and it has not yet been revealed what we shall be, but we know that when He is revealed, we shall be like Him, for we shall see Him as He is.
Eph 5:1-2 (verse 2)

Line: *I came to understand that He advocates for us with His whole being.*
Rom 8:34 Who is he who condemns? *It is* Christ who died, and furthermore is also risen, who is even at the right hand of God, who also makes intercession for us.
1 Tim 2:3-6 5 For there is one God and one mediator between God and men, the man Christ Jesus
Rom 8:31-35 (verse 34), Heb 4:14-16 (verse 15)

Sub-Title: His Face
Line: *His face was as if it were liquid crystal glass made up of pure love, light, and life. Jesus did have a face just like most humans, but it was changing into different human like faces.*
Luke 9:29-33 29 As He prayed, the appearance of His face was altered, and His robe became white and glistening.
Mark 16:12-13 (verse 12), Luke 24:28-34 (verses 30-32)

Line: *His face had the colors of the rainbow and colors I cannot describe inside it.*

Ezek 1:27-28 28 Like the appearance of a rainbow in the clouds on a rainy day, so was the radiance around him. This was the appearance of the likeness of the glory of the LORD. When I saw it, I fell facedown, and I heard the voice of one speaking.

Line: *They came out and off Him as the waves of the ocean coming on to the shore. I was seeing the colors and I was part of the colors.*
Rev 4:2-3 3 And the one who sat there had the appearance of jasper and carnelian. A rainbow, resembling an emerald, encircled the throne.

Line: *I was seeing Jesus, and I was a part of Jesus. I was in Jesus, and Jesus was shining out of me.*
John 14:19-24 20 At that day you will know that I *am* in My Father, and you in Me, and I in you.
Acts 9:3-4 (verse 3), Rev 1:9-20 (verse 16)

Line: *The brightness was around me. I was part of the brightness, and brightness was shining out of me.*
Rev 21:22-23 23 The city had no need of the sun or of the moon to shine in it, for the glory of God illuminated it. The Lamb is its light.
Rev 22:1-5 5 There shall be no night there: They need no lamp nor light of the sun, for the Lord God gives them light. And they shall reign forever and ever.
Eph 5:13-14 (verse 14)

Line: *On His head was a crown that looked like the sun in all its glory.*
Rev 19:11-13 12 His eyes were like a flame of fire, and on His head were many crowns. He had a name written that no one knew except Himself.
Rev 6:1-2 (verse 2), Rev 14:14-16 (verse 14)

Subtitle: His Head

Line: *This crown was really bright, with rays going up and out in the atmosphere of heaven.*

Isa 30:25-26 26 Moreover the light of the moon will be as the light of the sun, And the light of the sun will be sevenfold, As the light of seven days, In the day that the LORD binds up the bruise of His people And heals the stroke of their wound.

Read Isa 30:25-26 notes from the NET BIBLE at bible.org

Malachi 4:2-3, 2 But to you who fear My name The Sun of Righteousness shall arise With healing in His wings (warm rays); And you shall go out And grow fat like stall-fed calves.

Read Malachi 4:2-3 notes from the NET BIBLE at bible. org

Line: *The rays intertwine with His hair. His hair was like John said in Revelations.*

Rev 1:9-20 14 His head and hair were white like wool, as white as snow, and His eyes like a flame of fire

Daniel 7:9-10 (verse 9)

Subtitle: He Is Love

Line: *Everything about Him is love.*

1 John 4:16-17 16 And we have known and believed the love that God has for us. God is love, and he who abides in love abides in God, and God in him 17 Love has been perfected among us in this: that we may have boldness in the day of judgment; because as He is, so are we in this world.

1 John 4:7-12 (verse 8)

Line: *Yet you know in yourself that he loves all, but the love for you is so personal it seems as if it is only for you.*
Isa. 49:14-16 15 "Can a woman forget her nursing child, And not have compassion on the son of her womb? Surely they may forget, Yet I will not forget you.

Line: *You know He has cared for you forever and will care for you forever.*
Dan 7:21-27 22 until the Ancient of Days came, and a judgment was made in favor of the saints of the Most High, and the time came for the saints to possess the kingdom. 27 Then the kingdom and dominion, And the greatness of the kingdoms under the whole heaven, Shall be given to the people, the saints of the Most High. His kingdom is an everlasting kingdom, And all dominions shall serve and obey Him.'
Rev 21:2-4 3 And I heard a loud voice from heaven saying, "Behold, the tabernacle of God is with men, and He will dwell with them, and they shall be His people. God Himself will be with them and be their God.
Mat 11:11-12 (verse 11)

Chapter 7 Notes
What Did I See In Heaven?

Subtitle: None

Line: *When I died, I knew where to go. There was no one telling me where to go.*

John 14:1-4 4 And where I go you know, and the way you know.

Line: *Everything is alive and there is nothing dead there.*

Luke 12:32-34 33 Sell what you have and give alms; provide yourselves money bags which do not grow old, a treasure in the heavens that does not fail, where no thief approaches nor moth destroys.

Titus 1:1-3 (verse 2), Jam 1:12-13

Line: *I understood true death was not having the Father God or Jesus or the Holy Spirit in your life.*

Rev 21:6-8 8 But the cowardly, unbelieving, abominable, murderers, sexually immoral, sorcerers, idolaters, and all liars shall have their part in the lake which burns with fire and brimstone, which is the second death..

Rev 20:12-15 (verse 14)

Subtitle: Back From The Dead? - On The Contrary

Line: *No...I was alive with the Father and Son.*

Ps 36:7-9 9 For with You is the fountain of life; In Your light we see light.

Mat 22:29-32 32 'I am the God of Abraham, the God of Isaac, and the God of Jacob'? God is not the God of the dead, but of the living."

Heb 4:11-13 12 For the word of God is living and powerful, and sharper than any two-edged sword, piercing even to the division of soul and spirit, and of joints and marrow, and is a discerner of the thoughts and intents of the heart.

Line: *Our God is pure life, light, and love.*

LOVE

1 John 4:7-11 7 Beloved, let us love one another, for love is of God; and everyone who loves is born of God and knows God. 8 He who does not love does not know God, for God is love.

1 Cor 13:8-13 (verses 8,13), 1 John 4:15-16 (verse 16)

LIFE

Gen 2:7 And the LORD God formed man of the dust of the ground, and breathed into his nostrils the breath of life; and man became a living being.

John 5:24-27 (verse 26)

LIGHT

Ps 36:7-9 9 For with You is the fountain of life; In Your light we see light.

Ps 104:1-2 2 Who cover Yourself with light as with a garment, Who stretch out the heavens like a curtain.

Ps 119:129-132 130 The entrance of Your words gives light; It gives understanding to the simple.

2 Cor 4:5-6 (verse 6)

Line: *As I said earlier, everything in heaven is alive. The light-like buildings (they looked like light but were not light), the landscape, and atmosphere, I mean everything.*

Rev 16:4-7 7 And I heard another from the altar saying, "Even so, Lord God Almighty, true and righteous are Your judgments."

Read Rev 16:7 from the NET BIBLE at bible.org

Rev 19:4-6 5 Then a voice came from the throne, saying, "Praise our God, all you His servants and those who fear Him, both small and great!

Line: *As I said earlier, everything in heaven is alive. **The light-like buildings** (they looked like light but were not light), the landscape, and atmosphere, I mean everything.*

Rev 21:10-23 10 And he carried me away in the Spirit to a great and high mountain, and showed me the great city, the holy Jerusalem, descending out of heaven from God, 11 having the glory of God. Her light was like a most precious stone, like a jasper stone, clear as crystal. 21 The twelve gates were twelve pearls: each individual gate was of one pearl. And the street of the city was pure gold, like transparent glass. 23 The city had no need of the sun or of the moon to shine in it, for the glory of God illuminated it. The Lamb is its light.
Isa 44:21-23 (verse 23), Isa 55:11-12 (verse 12)

Line: *As I said earlier, everything in heaven is alive. The light-like buildings (they looked like light but were not light), the landscape, and atmosphere, I mean everything.*
Job 38:33-36 35 Can you send out lightnings, that they may go, And say to you, 'Here we are!'?
Rev 10:3-4 3 and cried with a loud voice, as when a lion roars. When he cried out, seven thunders uttered their voices.

Line: *Because of coming from earth and living with death, a thought went through my thinking, "Aren't we going to run out of room, because there is no death and everything keeps on living?"*
1 Tim 6:11-14 13 I urge you in the sight of God who gives life to all things, and before Christ Jesus who witnessed the good confession before Pontius Pilate.
Ezek 18:30-32 32 For I have no pleasure in the death of one who dies," says the Lord GOD. "Therefore turn and live!"
Gen 1:11-13 (verse 11), Gen 1:20-24 (verses 20, 24), Gen 2:7, Ps 115:14-15 (verse 15)

Subtitle: Heaven Is Huge

Line: *Heaven is big, large, huge, extensive, spacious and expanding.*

Eccl 3:13-14 14 I know that whatever God does, It shall be forever. Nothing can be added to it, And nothing taken from it. God does it, that men should fear before Him.

2 Cor 3:17-18 (verse 18), 2 Cor 4:16-18

Line: *All I can tell people is that where God is, IS BIG!*

Ps 40:5 Many, O LORD my God, are Your wonderful works Which You have done; And Your thoughts toward us Cannot be recounted to You in order; If I would declare and speak of them, They are more than can be numbered.

Ps 111:2-4, Ps 115:15-16 (verse 15), Ps 123:1

Subtitle: Distance And Time

Line: *If I wanted to be somewhere else in heaven I just had to think it and I was there.*

Act 8:38-40 39 Now when they came up out of the water, the Spirit of the Lord caught Philip away, so that the eunuch saw him no more; and he went on his way rejoicing.

Ezek 3:11-15 (verses 12-14), John 6:15-21 (verse 21)

Line: *I know I will outlast every problem that comes my way and some day soon, I will be with Jesus.*

Ps 90:3-6 4 For a thousand years in Your (God) sight Are like yesterday when it is past, And like a watch in the night.

Ps 102:23-28 (verse 24), 2 Pet 3:8-9 (verse 8)

Line: *Why would you put time on eternity? Why do we put time on earth?*

Gen 8:20-22 22 "While the earth remains, Seedtime and harvest, Cold and heat, Winter and summer, And day and night Shall not cease."

Gen 1:14-19 (verse 14)

Subtitle: The Atmosphere In Heaven

Line: *Jesus and the Father light up everything; there is no darkness in heaven.*

Rev 22:4-5 5 There shall be no night there: They need no lamp nor light of the sun, for the Lord God gives them light. And they shall reign forever and ever.

Isa 60:19-20 (verse 19), 2 Cor 4:5-6 (verse 6)

Line: *It is a golden, yellow, white. An artist that I know says it sounds like sunrise colors.*

Job 37:21-23 22 He comes from the north as golden splendor; With God is awesome majesty.

Read Job 37:21-23 notes from the NET BIBLE at bible.org

Subtitle: The Colors In Heaven

Line: *The colors of flowers here on earth, are the closest to the colors I experienced in heaven and yet they have lost their glory compared to the colors in heaven.*

Mat 6:28-30 28 "So why do you worry about clothing? Consider the lilies of the field, how they grow: they neither toil nor spin; 29 and yet I say to you that even Solomon in all his glory was not arrayed like one of these. 30 Now if God so clothes the grass of the field, which today is, and tomorrow is thrown into the oven, will He not much more clothe you, O you of little faith?

Luke 12:27-28 (verse 27)

Subtitle: Jesus' Words Are Alive

Line: *His voice left Him with power and authority, but when it got to me, it was life, and comfort.*

Ps 107:20 He sent his word, and healed them, and delivered them from their destructions.

Rev 1:9-20 (verses 10,12)

Line: *I felt that speaking words there were a waste of energy, or just not important.*

Eccl 5:6-7 7 For in the multitude of dreams and many words there is also vanity. But fear God.

Subtitle: Communication In Heaven

Line: *I understand that, but in heaven, Jesus and the Father thought something and it was transferred to me. The other beings thought it and it was transferred to me.*

Acts 16:6-10 9 And a vision appeared to Paul in the night. A man of Macedonia stood and pleaded with him, saying, "Come over to Macedonia and help us." 10 Now after he had seen the vision, immediately we sought to go to Macedonia, concluding that the Lord had called us to preach the gospel to them.

Acts 27: 9-12 (verse 10)

Line: *Because everything is alive they could all communicate with you.*

Rev 4:6-8 7 The first living creature was like a lion, the second living creature like a calf, the third living creature had a face like a man, and the fourth living creature was like a flying eagle. 8 The four living creatures, each having six wings, were full of eyes around and within. And they do not rest day or night, saying: Holy, holy, holy, Lord God Almighty, Who was and is and is to come!" 9 Whenever the living creatures give glory and honor and thanks to Him who sits on the throne, who lives forever and ever, 11 "You are worthy, O Lord, To receive glory and honor and power; For You created all things, And by Your will they exist and were created."

Rev 8:12-13 (verse 13) Read Rev 8:13 from the NET BIBLE at bible.org, Rev 10:2-4, (verses 3-4), Rev16:4-7 (verse 7) Read Rev 16:7 from the NET BIBLE at bible.org

Line: *Everything was RIGHT, so there was no miscommunication with each other.*
Col 4:2-6 5 Walk in wisdom toward those who are outside, redeeming the time. 6 Let your speech always be with grace, seasoned with salt, that you may know how you ought to answer each one.

Line: *There was nothing you would have to hide from each other. We all had pure thoughts and every thought was pure.*
Phil 4:7-9 8 Finally, brethren, whatever things are true, whatever things are noble, whatever things are just, whatever things are pure, whatever things are lovely, whatever things are of good report, if there is any virtue and if there is anything praiseworthy—meditate on these things.
Gen 2:23-25 (verse 25), Gen 3:4-7 (verse 7)

Line: *There was a rule that you did not go into any of heavenly creation's thoughts without them giving you permission to.*
1 Cor 6:12 All things are lawful for me, but all things are not helpful. All things are lawful for me, but I will not be brought under the power of any.
1 Cor 8:8-9, verse 9

Line: *The last being (Satan) that did that is no longer there in heaven. What power we could all have if we just really understood what thinking could do.*
Isa 14:12-1, 12 "How you are fallen from heaven, O Lucifer, son of the morning! How you are cut down to the ground, You who weakened the nations! 15 Yet you shall be brought down to Sheol, To the lowest depths of the Pit.
Ezek. 28:14-17, verse 17, Luke 10:17-20, verse 18

Subtitle: Everyone And Everything Praised The Lord
Line: *Every part of God's creation praises God all the time, and no one else receives praise, but only God.*
Isa 42:5-9 8 I am the LORD, that is My name; And My glory I will not give to another, Nor My praise to carved images.
Ex 20:2-6 (verses 3-5), Luke 4:5-8 (verse 8), Rev 21:22-27 (verse 22)

Line: *There is a part of being there, that you knew that is what you do.*
Ps146:1-2 1 Praise the LORD! Praise the LORD, O my soul! 2 While I live I will praise the LORD; I will sing praises to my God while I have my being.
Ps 148:1-7 (verse 1), Ps 149:1-9 (verse 1), Ps 150:1-6 (verse 2)

Line: *To hear the flowers praise the Lord is wonderful. The birds sing praise to the Lord. Water praised the Lord. Mountains praised the Lord. Praise came from the atmosphere. Praise was in the atmosphere. Praise was the atmosphere. We all praised Him repeatedly, over and over again.*
Ps 148:1-14 1 Praise the LORD! Praise the LORD from the heavens; Praise Him in the heights! 2 Praise Him, all His angels; Praise Him, all His hosts! 3 Praise Him, sun and moon; Praise Him, all you stars of light! 4 Praise Him, you heavens of heavens, And you waters above the heavens! 5 Let them praise the name of the LORD, For He commanded and they were created. 6 He also established them forever and ever; He made a decree which shall not pass away. Praise the LORD from the earth, You great sea creatures and all the depths; 8 Fire and hail, snow and clouds; Stormy wind, fulfilling His word; 9 Mountains and all hills; Fruitful trees and all cedars; 10 Beasts and all cattle; Creeping things and flying fowl; 11 Kings of the earth and all peoples; Princes

and all judges of the earth; 12 Both young men and maidens; Old men and children. 13 Let them praise the name of the LORD, For His name alone is exalted; His glory *is* above the earth and heaven. 14 And He has exalted the horn of His people, The praise of all His saints Of the children of Israel, A people near to Him. Praise the LORD!

Line: *Just writing this down reminds me of the fact, that praise did not leave my thinking when I was there.*
John 4:23-24 23 But the hour is coming, and now is, when the true worshipers will worship the Father in spirit and truth; for the Father is seeking such to worship Him. 24 God is Spirit, and those who worship Him must worship in spirit and truth."
Mat 21:15-16 (verse 16), Phil 3:17-21 (verses 20-21)

Subtitle: Our Connection In Heaven
Line: *God connects every one of His creations together.*
2 Cor 12:4-26 6 And there are diversities of activities, but it is the same God who works all in all. 11 But one and the same Spirit works all these things, distributing to each one individually as He wills. 12 For as the body is one and has many members, but all the members of that one body, being many, are one body, so also is Christ. 13 For by one Spirit we were all baptized into one body—whether Jews or Greeks, whether slaves or free—and have all been made to drink into one Spirit. 18 But now God has set the members, each one of them, in the body just as He pleased. 20 But now indeed there are many members, yet one body. 25 that there should be no schism in the body, but that the members should have the same care for one another. 26 And if one member suffers, all the members suffer with it; or if one member is honored, all the members rejoice with it
Rom 15:5-6, Col 2:1-3 (verses 2-3)

Subtitle: Relating My Experience To You

Line: *There is no sin to corrupt what God has made.*

Rev 21:22-27 27 But there shall by no means enter it anything that defiles, or causes an abomination or a lie, but only those who are written in the Lamb's Book of Life.

Chapter 9 Notes
The True Gatekeeper Of Heaven

Subtitle: None

Line: *I came to understand who the real gatekeeper of Heaven is, it is only Jesus.*

John 6:38-40 40 And this is the will of Him who sent Me, that everyone who sees the Son and believes in Him may have everlasting life; and I will raise him up at the last day."

John 10:14-16 (verses 15-16), 2 Peter 3:8-9 (verse 9)

Subtitle: I Looked Into Jesus' Eyes

Line: *His eyes are like flames of fire with changing colors of red, orange, blue, green, yellow, and many other colors. John said in Revelations 1:14 that, "His eyes (are) like a flame of fire"*

Rev 1:12-14 14 His head and hair were white like wool, as white as snow, and His eyes like a flame of fire;

Rev 2:18-19 (verse 18), Rev 19:11-14 (verse 12)

Line: *I saw in His eyes that He wanted everyone there, who is still alive on this earth.*

1 Tim 2:1-4 1 Therefore I exhort first of all that supplications, prayers, intercessions, and giving of thanks be made for all men, 3 For this is good and acceptable in the sight of God our Savior, 4 who desires all men to be saved and to come to the knowledge of the truth.

Isa 55:6-7 (verse 7), Luke 5:29-32 (verses 31-32)

Line: *Then His eyes looked at me with the fiery red flame and said, "WHO ARE YOU TO NULIFY WHAT I HAD DONE!"*

Rom 5:6-11 6 For when we were still without strength, in due time Christ died for the ungodly. 8 But God demonstrates His own love toward us, in that while we were still sinners, Christ died for us. 9 Much more then, having now been justified by His blood, we shall be saved from wrath through Him. 10 For if when we were enemies we were reconciled to God through the death of His Son, much more, having been reconciled, we shall be saved by His life. 11 And not only that, but we also rejoice in God through our Lord Jesus Christ, through whom we have now received the reconciliation.

Rom 4:24-25 (verse 25), Rom 6:3-10 (verses 4,8-10), Gal 1:3-5 (verse 4), Eph 2:1-10 (verses 1,4-6,8,10)

Chapter 11 Notes
Jesus Wants All People Saved

Subtitle: None

Line: *He was strategizing.*

Pr 19:20-21 21 There are many plans in a man's heart, Nevertheless the LORD's counsel—that will stand.

2 Chro 20:13-17 (verses 14-17), Isa 9:6-7 (verse 6), Read Isa 9:6-7 notes from the NET BIBLE at bible.org, Isa 55:8-9

Line: *He was strategizing to get more people on this earth to know Him as Lord and Savior.*

Mat 9:35-38 36 But when He saw the multitudes, He was moved with compassion for them, because they were weary and scattered, like sheep having no shepherd. 37 Then He said to His disciples, "The harvest truly is plentiful, but the laborers are few. 38 Therefore pray the Lord of the harvest to send out laborers into His harvest."

Mat 18:10-14 (verses 10-11,14), Luke 15:1-10 (verses 1-2,7,10), John 6:35-47 (verses 37,39-40,44,47-48)

Line: *God is using everything that he can, short of evil, to get people to know Jesus as Lord and Savior.*

Ezek 18:30-32 32 For I have no pleasure in the death of one who dies," says the Lord GOD. "Therefore turn and live!"

Ps 111:9, John 6:43-44 (verse 44)

Line: *He is looking for people on earth to work with Him in getting people to know who He is.*

Ezek 22:30-31 30 So I sought for a man among them who would make a wall, and stand in the gap before Me on behalf of the land, that I should not destroy it; but I found no one.

1 Sam 13:13-14 (verse 14), Dan 9:2-3 (verse 3)

Line: *He is urging all of mankind to press into the Kingdom of God.*
Luke 16:16-17 16 "The law and the prophets were until John. Since that time the kingdom of God has been preached, and everyone is pressing into it.
Eph 4:1-3 (verses 1,3), 1 Thes 2:10-12 (verse 11)

Line: *We are so very important to Him!*
Mat 10:29-31 30 But the very hairs of your head are all numbered. 31 Do not fear therefore; you are of more value than many sparrows.
Luke 12:4-7 (verse 6), Rom 8: 18-30 (verse 30)

Line: *I understood just how important we that are on earth are to Him.*
Dan 4:1-3 4 I Nebuchadnezzar the king, To all peoples, nations, and languages that dwell in all the earth: Peace be multiplied to you. I thought it good to declare the signs and wonders that the Most High God has worked for me.
John 3:1-18 (verses 16-17), 1 Tim 2:1-4

Subtitle: Heavenly Interventions
Line: *However, when I look throughout the New Testament there is more than once, times where Jesus is sending angels on what I call "heavenly interventions" to get people saved every day.*
Acts 8:26-40 26 Now an angel of the Lord spoke to Philip, saying, "Arise and go toward the south along the road which goes down from Jerusalem to Gaza." This is desert.
Acts 10:1-48 3 About the ninth hour of the day he saw clearly in a vision an angel of God coming in and saying to him, "Cornelius!"
Acts 12:5-19 (verse 7)

Line: *As soon as someone turns to God in his or her heart, He is right there.*
Dan 10:10-21 12 Then he said to me, "Do not fear, Daniel, for from the first day that you set your heart to understand, and to humble yourself before your God, your words were heard; and I have come because of your words.

Line: *I tell others there are many people there that we did not think would be there.*
Rom 14:1-4 4 Who are you to judge another's servant? To his own master he stands or falls. Indeed, he will be made to stand, for God is able to make him stand.
Mat 22:1-14, (verses 8-9), John 10:22-30 (verses 27-28)

Line: *Also, there are those who we thought would be there, but are not.*
Mat 22:1-13 11 "But when the king came in to see the guests, he saw a man there who did not have on a wedding garment. 12 So he said to him, 'Friend, how did you come in here without a wedding garment?' And he was speechless. 13 Then the king said to the servants, 'Bind him hand and foot, take him away, and cast *him* into outer darkness; there will be weeping and gnashing of teeth.'
Mat 23:27-28, Rom 11:19-36 (verses 20-21)

Line: *As it says in Romans chapter 10, God is looking at a person's heart - not just what they say or do.*
Rom 10:1-13 9 that if you confess with your mouth the Lord Jesus and believe in your heart that God has raised Him from the dead, you will be saved. 10 For with the heart one believes unto righteousness, and with the mouth confession is made unto salvation.
Luke 6:46-49 (verse 48), John 2:23-25 (verses 24-25)

Line: *Everything is right and everyone has the right to be in a place of rightness.*
Rom 10:1-13 4 For Christ *is* the end of the law for righteousness to everyone who believes.
Ps 119:137-144 (verse 144), 2 Cor 5:12-21 (verse 21)

Line: *Everything there is alive and everyone has a right to live with God forever.*
John 3:1-21 17 For God did not send His Son into the world to condemn the world, but that the world through Him might be saved.
John 5:24-30 (verse 24), John 17:20-26 (verse 24)

Subtitle: The Army Of God
Line: *There is a heavenly unit and earthly unit, but they are the same army of God.*
1 Sam 17:1-58 45 Then David said to the Philistine, "You come to me with a sword, with a spear, and with a javelin. But I come to you in the name of the LORD of hosts, the God of the armies of Israel, whom you have defied. 46 This day the LORD will deliver you into my hand, and I will strike you and take your head from you. And this day I will give the carcasses of the camp of the Philistines to the birds of the air and the wild beasts of the earth, that all the earth may know that there is a God in Israel.
Gen 3:1-24 (verse 24), Eph 6:10-12 (verse 12)

Line: *The heavenly unit is made up of the angels of God.*
Mat 26:48-54 53 Or do you think that I cannot now pray to My Father, and He will provide Me with more than twelve legions (72 Thousand Angels) of angels?
2 King 6:8-23 (verse 17), Dan 4:34-36 (verse 35)

Line: *They understood whose government they belong to.*
Dan 7:9-14 13 I was watching in the night visions, And behold, One like the Son of Man, Coming with the clouds of heaven! He came to the Ancient of Days, And they brought Him near before Him. 14 Then to Him was given dominion and glory and a kingdom, That all peoples, nations, and languages should serve Him. His dominion is an everlasting dominion, Which shall not pass away, And His kingdom the one Which shall not be destroyed.
Dan 2:24-45 (verses 44-45), Mat 18;10-14 (verse 10)

Line: *They understood whose Kingdom they work for.*
Mat 13:36-43 41 The Son of Man will send out His angels, and they will gather out of His kingdom all things that offend, and those who practice lawlessness, 42 and will cast them into the furnace of fire. There will be wailing and gnashing of teeth.
Heb 12:25-29 (verse 28), Rev 19:11-16 (verse 14)

Line: *When Jesus would communicate to them, they showed great AWE (respect).*
1 Pet 3:18-22. 22 who has gone into heaven and is at the right hand of God, angels and authorities and powers having been made subject to Him.
Ps 89:5-7 (verse 5), Isa 6:1-3 (verse 2)

Line: *I wanted to be with His creation that respected Him for who He is - King of Kings and Lord of Lords.*
Rev 19:11-16 16 And He has on *His* robe and on His thigh a name written: KING OF KINGS AND LORD OF LORDS.
Pr 19:12-25 (verse 23), Phil 2:5-11 (verses 9-11)

Line: *I saw how those heavenly creatures would bow before they left Him, and back out as they left.*

Ps 89:1-18 7 God is greatly to be feared (respect) in the assembly of the saints (Angels), And to be held in reverence by all those around Him.
Zech 6:1-8 (verses 5-7)

Line: *They left right and fast on to the assignment He sent them on.*
Joel 2:5-11 7 They (Angels) run like mighty men, They climb the wall like men of war; Every one marches in formation, And they do not break ranks. 8 They do not push one another; Every one marches in his own column. Though they lunge between the weapons, They are not cut down.
Dan 10:10-24 (verse 11), Luke 2:8-14, (verses 9-10,13-14)

Line: *He sent them on.*
Mat 24:29-31 31 And He will send His angels with a great sound of a trumpet, and they will gather together His elect from the four winds, from one end of heaven to the other.
Luke 1:1-25 (verse 19)

Line: *I did not see one of them question anything He commanded them to do.*
Jude 1:5-10 9 Yet Michael the archangel, in contending with the devil, when he disputed about the body of Moses, dared not bring against him a reviling accusation, but said, "The Lord rebuke you!"
Luke 1:5-25 (verses 19-20)

Line: *They were sent to fight in the heavenlies.*
2 Sam 5:17-25 23 Therefore David inquired of the LORD, and He said, "You shall not go up; circle around behind them, and come upon them in front of the mulberry trees. 24 And it shall be, when you hear the sound of marching in the tops of the mulberry trees, then you shall advance quickly.

For then the LORD will go out before you to strike the camp of the Philistines."
Dan 10:10-21 (verse 13), Rev 12:7-12 (verse 7)

Line: *They were fighting evil spirits that belong to Satan's army.*
Eph 6:10-20 12 For we do not wrestle against flesh and blood, but against principalities, against powers, against the rulers of the darkness of this age, against spiritual hosts of wickedness in the heavenly places.
Dan 10:1-21 (verses 20-21)

Line: *I knew that prayer is what moved them.*
Mat 9:35-38 37 Then He said to His disciples, "The harvest truly *is* plentiful, but the laborers *are* few. 38 Therefore pray the Lord of the harvest to send out laborers into His harvest."
2 Chr 7:12-21 (verses 14-15), Mat 6:5-13 (verses 8-10)

Line: *Then, there was the earthly unit.*
1 Sam 17:1-58 26 Then David spoke to the men who stood by him, saying, "What shall be done for the man who kills this Philistine and takes away the reproach from Israel? For who *is* this uncircumcised Philistine, that he should defy the armies of the living God?" 45 Then David said to the Philistine, "You come to me with a sword, with a spear, and with a javelin. But I come to you in the name of the LORD of hosts, the God of the armies of Israel, whom you have defied.
Eph 6:10-20 (verses 10-11)

Line: *When Jesus told me to "Go Back", on the inside of me, I knew he was saying, "I need you there more than here," and I left as a soldier going to war.*
Mat 28:16-20 19 Go therefore and make disciples of all the nations, baptizing them in the name of the Father and of the

Son and of the Holy Spirit, 20 teaching them to observe all things that I have commanded you; and lo, I am with you always, even to the end of the age." Amen.
Col 4:1-10 (verse 2)

Line: *I knew that it would be for a short time and my life on this earth will be short lived.*
Ps 39:4-6 5 Indeed, You have made my days *as* handbreadths, And my age *is* as nothing before You; Certainly every man at his best state *is* but vapor. Selah
Phil 3:17-20 (verse 20), Heb 11:13-16 (verse 13)

Line: *I know what the heart of God is. It is to get people saved. To get people to live with Him forever.*
John 3:1-12 16 For God so loved the world that He gave His only begotten Son, that whoever believes in Him should not perish but have everlasting life.
2 Cor 12-20 (verse 14), 1 John 3:1-3 (verse 1)

Subtitle: God's Army On Earth
Line: *First of all, this unit loves God with all their being.*
Ps 31:21-24 23 Oh, love the LORD, all you His saints! For the LORD preserves the faithful, And fully repays the proud person.
Mat 22:34-40 37 Jesus said to him, You shall love the LORD your God with all your heart, with all your soul, and with all your mind.
John 14:15-18 (verse 15)

Line: *These are they that say Jesus is Lord and Savior.*
Mat 16:24-27 24 Then Jesus said to His disciples, "If anyone desires to come after Me, let him deny himself, and take up his cross, and follow Me.
Col 3:12-17 (verses 12-13)

Line: *They know who sent them.*
John 15:9-17 16 You did not choose Me, but I chose you and appointed you that you should go and bear fruit, and *that* your fruit should remain, that whatever you ask the Father in My name He may give you. 17 These things I command you, that you love one another.
Mat 23:1-36 (verses 11-12), 1 Thess 3:11-13 (verse 11)

Line: *These have come to an understanding of His authority and whose authority they have.*
John 14:12-14 12 "Most assuredly, I say to you, he who believes in Me (Jesus), the works that I do he will do also; and greater works than these he will do, because I go to My Father. 13 And whatever you ask in My name, that I will do, that the Father may be glorified in the Son. 14 If you ask anything in My name, I will do it.

Line: *They know there is a war going on with Satan and his fallen angels.*
Eph 6:10-20 11 Put on the whole armor of God, that you may be able to stand against the wiles of the devil. 12 For we do not wrestle against flesh and blood, but against principalities, against powers, against the rulers of the darkness of this age, against spiritual hosts of wickedness in the heavenly places.
Mat 10:34-39 (verse 34), 1 Pet 5:6-11 (verse 8)

Line: *They know their weapons and use them in battles they encounter.*
2 Cor 10:1-6 3 For though we walk in the flesh, we do not war according to the flesh. 4 For the weapons of our warfare *are* not carnal but mighty in God for pulling down strongholds, 5 casting down arguments and every high thing that exalts itself against the knowledge of God, bringing every thought into captivity to the obedience of Christ
Mat 10:1-4 (verse 1), Rom 12:3-8 (verse 3)

Line: *They have a great understanding of whose government and kingdom they are under and belong to.*
Eph 2:19-22 20 having been built on the foundation of the apostles and prophets, Jesus Christ Himself being the chief cornerstone, 21 in whom the whole building, being fitted together, grows into a holy temple in the Lord, 22 in whom you also are being built together for a dwelling place of God in the Spirit.
Ps 47:8-9 (verse 8), John 12:44-50 (verses 49-50)

Line: *They spend a lot of time with the Father in His Word (Bible) and prayer.*
Mat 26:36-46 41 Watch and pray, lest you enter into temptation. The spirit indeed *is* willing, but the flesh *is* weak.
2 Tim 2:14-26 15 Be diligent to present yourself approved to God, a worker who does not need to be ashamed, rightly dividing the word of truth.
1 Thess 5:12-20 17 pray without ceasing,

Line: *By doing this they are able to hear His commandment, when He commands them to do something.*
John 10:20-30 27 My sheep hear My voice, and I know them, and they follow Me.
Eph 2:14-18 (verse 18)

Line: *They understand that when Jesus or the Father through the Holy Spirit asks them to do something for the Kingdom, it is a command and not a request.*
1 John 3:16-24 22 And whatever we ask we receive from Him, because we keep His commandments and do those things that are pleasing in His sight. 23 And this is His commandment: that we should believe on the name of His Son Jesus Christ and love one another, as He gave us commandment. 24 Now he who keeps His commandments abides in Him,

and He in him. And by this we know that He abides in us, by the Spirit whom He has given us.
John 15:9-17 (verse 14), John 10:7-21 (verse 18)

Line: *These have come to know their purpose on this earth and accept it.*
Heb 10:19-25 24 And let us consider one another in order to stir up love and good works, 25 not forsaking the assembling of ourselves together, as *is* the manner of some, but exhorting *one another,* and so much the more as you see the Day approaching.
Rom 15:1-6 (verse 2), Gal 6:1-5 (verses 1-2)

Line: *They are willing to lose their lives here on earth for Him.*
John 12:20-26 25 He who loves his life will lose it, and he who hates his life in this world will keep it for eternal life.
Mat 19:20-22 (verse 21), Mat 20:24-28 (verses 26-27)

Line: *They know that they are part of a bigger army and have a God that will not leave them alone.*
Mat 18:15-20 20 For where two or three are gathered together in My name, I am there in the midst of them.
Ps 78:12-16 (verse 12), Mat 11:25-30 (verse 30)

Line: *I came to understand that I was not being sent out alone with a heavy load.*
Rom 8:31-37 31 What then shall we say to these things? If God *is* for us, who *can be* against us? 32 He who did not spare His own Son, but delivered Him up for us all, how shall He not with Him also freely give us all things?
Heb 12:1-2, Heb 13:1-6 (verses 5-6)

Chapter 13 Notes
What Jesus Told Me About Our Churches

Subtitle: Two Spirits In The Church

Line: *First, He let me know that there are two spirits (attitudes) in our churches today.*

1 John 4:4-6 6 We are of God. He who knows God hears us; he who is not of God does not hear us. By this we know the spirit of truth and the spirit of error.

Line: *He let me know that His church is not one denomination against another.*

Eph 6:10-20 12 For we do not wrestle against flesh and blood, but against principalities, against powers, against the rulers of the darkness of this age, against spiritual hosts of wickedness in the heavenly places.

Line: *As long as someone follows Romans 10:9-10, they are in.*

Rom 10:8-10 9 that if you confess with your mouth the Lord Jesus and believe in your heart that God has raised Him from the dead, you will be saved. 10 For with the heart one believes unto righteousness, and with the mouth confession is made unto salvation.

Line: *What comes with this, is love for God and love for others.*

1 John 4:17-19 17 Love has been perfected among us in this: that we may have boldness in the day of judgment; because as He is, so are we in this world.

1 John 3:1-3 (verse 3), 1 John 3:10-15 (verse 11)

Subtitle: We Are One Body

Line: *We do meet in different buildings, but He sees everyone who has accepted Jesus as Lord and Savor as in His church.*

1 John 4:1-3 2 By this you know the Spirit of God: Every spirit that confesses that Jesus Christ has come in the flesh is of God, 3 and every spirit that does not confess that Jesus Christ has come in the flesh is not of God. And this is the spirit of the Antichrist, which you have heard was coming, and is now already in the world.

Mat 16:13-20 (verse 18), Acts 2:46-47 (verse 47), Eph 5:22-32 (verse 27), 1 John 4:1-3 (verse 2)

Line: *He also wants all of us to belong to a local body of believers so we can build each other up for the work He has set before us.*

Heb 10:19-15 24 And let us consider one another in order to stir up love and good works, 25 not forsaking the assembling of ourselves together, as *is* the manner of some, but exhorting *one another,* and so much the more as you see the Day approaching.

Eph 4:11-16 (verse 11), 1 John 1:1-10 (verses 3,7)

Line: *I am talking about those who believe in Jesus as the Son of God and have made Him Lord and Savior of their lives.*

1 John 4:1-3 2 By this you know the Spirit of God: Every spirit that confesses that Jesus Christ has come in the flesh is of God, 3 and every spirit that does not confess that Jesus Christ has come in the flesh is not of God. And this is the spirit of the Antichrist, which you have heard was coming, and is now already in the world.

1 John 3:4-10 (verse 9), 1 John 2:3-6 (verse 5), 1 John 2:20-23 (verse 23)

Line: *People that believe, that God the Father, sent His son into the world to save it, to save you, to save people.*
John 3:1-21 17 For God did not send His Son into the world to condemn the world, but that the world through Him might be saved.
Eph 2:11-22 (verse 13)

Line: ***Those that believe that the Holy Spirit, Jesus and the Father are one and that there is only one true God,*** *the one who made man, not a man made God.*
John 14:15-18 17 the Spirit of truth, whom the world cannot receive, because it neither sees Him nor knows Him; but you know Him, for He dwells with you and will be in you. 18 I will not leave you orphans; I will come to you.
John 17:6-19 11 Now I am no longer in the world, but these are in the world, and I come to You. Holy Father, keep through Your name those whom You have given Me, that they may be one as We are.
John 1:1-5 (verse 1), John 10:25-30 (verse 30), Col 2:8-10 (verse 9)

Line: *Those that believe that Holy Spirit, Jesus and the Father are one and that there is only one true God**, the one who made man,** not a man made God.*
Gen 1:26-28 27 So God created man in His *own* image; in the image of God He created him; male and female He created them.
Gen 5:1-5 (verse 2), 1 Cor 11:1-16 (verse 12)

Line: *Those that believe that Holy Spirit, Jesus and the Father are one and that there is only one true God**, the one who made man, **not a man made God.***
Rom 1:18-25 22 Professing to be wise, they became fools, 23 and changed the glory of the incorruptible God into an

image made like corruptible man — and birds and four-footed animals and creeping things.
Ps 106:19-21 (verse 19), Isa 19:1-16 (verse 1)

Line: *Everyone who believes that Jesus is the Christ has been fathered by God (1John 5:1).*
1 John 5:1-5 1 Whoever believes that Jesus is the Christ is born of God, and everyone who loves Him who begot also loves him who is begotten of Him. 4 For whatever is born of God overcomes the world. And this is the victory that has overcome the world our faith.
1 John 2: 18-29 (verses 23,29)

Line: *He wants us to follow His Government/Kingdom rules on how to confront, correct or deal with each other.*
Mat 18:15-35 15 Moreover if your brother sins against you, go and tell him his fault between you and him alone. If he hears you, you have gained your brother. 16 But if he will not hear, take with you one or two more, that 'by the mouth of two or three witnesses every word may be established.
1 Cor 6:1-11 (verse 1)

Subtitle: The First Spirit
Line: *This spirit has the will to serve others first.*
Mart 25:34-40 40 And the King will answer and say to them, 'Assuredly, I say to you, inasmuch as you did *it* to one of the least of these My brethren, you did *it* to Me.
Phil 2:5-8 (verse 8)

Line: *Those who have this spirit keep God's Word at all cost.*
John 14:22-31 23 Jesus answered and said to him, "If anyone loves Me, he will keep My word; and My Father will love him, and We will come to him and make Our home with him.
John 8:31-32 (verse 31), Heb 10:23-25 (verse 23)

Line: *They have not denied His Name.*
2 Tim 2:11-15 11 This is a faithful saying: For if we died with Him, We shall also live with Him.
Mat 10:23-33 (verse 32), 1 Tim 1:18-19 (verse 19)

Line: ***They also know His Word is the Word of persever-*** ***ance,*** *in which He keeps them from the hour of testing.*
1 John 5:1-19 4 For whatever is born of God overcomes the world. And this is the victory that has overcome the world—our faith.
Ps 73:25-26 (verse 26), Isa 40:27-31 (verse 31)

Line: *They also know His Word is the Word of perseverance,* ***in which He keeps them from the hour of testing.***
Heb 13:1-6 5 Let your conduct be without covetousness; be content with such things as you have. For He Himself has said, "I will never leave you nor forsake you."
Rom 8:31-35 (verse 35), 1 John 5:18-21 (verse 18)

Line: *They are holding fast to what they know.*
Luke 12:8-12 8 Also I say to you, whoever confesses Me before men, him the Son of Man also will confess before the angels of God.
John 6:22-27 (verse 27), 1 Tim 6:18-19 (verse 19)

Line: *Those that have this spirit have a crown that no one can take from them, they can give it away, but no one can take it.*
1 Tim 4:6-8 8 Finally, there is laid up for me the crown of righteousness, which the Lord, the righteous Judge, will give to me on that Day, and not to me only but also to all who have loved His appearing.
Ps 5:11-12 (verse 12), Mat 5:5-10 (verse 10)

Line: *They are truly overcoming all that they face on this earth.*
Luke 12:46-49 48 He is like a man building a house, who dug deep and laid the foundation on the rock. And when the flood arose, the stream beat vehemently against that house, and could not shake it, for it was founded on the rock.
Ps 37:27-28 (verse 28), Rom 15:1-6 (verse 4)

Line: *They will be made a pillar in God's temple and will not go out from the temple of God.*
John 12:24-26 25 He who loves his life will lose it, and he who hates his life in this world will keep it for eternal life.
John 14:1-6 (verse 3), Luke 12:35-38 (verse 37)

Line: *They will have the name of God written on them along with the name of the city of God on them.*
Rev 14:1-5 1 Then I looked, and behold, a Lamb standing on Mount Zion, and with Him one hundred *and* forty-four thousand, having His Father's name written on their foreheads.

Subtitle: The Second Spirit
Line: *It has everything to do with a person's heart.*
John 2:23-25 25 and had no need that anyone should testify of man, for He knew what was in man.
Ps 69:5-12 (verse 5), Mat 15:15-21 (verse 19)

Line: *This spirit is neither cold or hot.*
Mat 15:1-9 8 These people draw near to Me with their mouth, And honor Me with their lips, But their heart is far from Me. 9 And in vain they worship Me, Teaching as doctrines the commandments of men.
Cor 10:14-22 (verse 21)

Line: *Because they are lukewarm He is going to spit (Greek: vomit) them out of His mouth.*

Lev 18:1-30 28 lest the land vomit you out also when you defile it, as it vomited out the nations that *were* before you.
Ps 119:17-27 (verse 21)

Line: *They that have this spirit say they are rich, wealthy and need nothing.*
Jer 9:23-24 23 Thus says the LORD: "Let not the wise man glory in his wisdom, Let not the mighty man glory in his might, Nor let the rich man glory in his riches;
Ps 49:5-12 (verses 6-7), 1 John 2:15-17 (verse 15)

Line: *Their problem is God knows their heart, He knows which spirit they have.*
1 Sam 16:6-13 7 But the LORD said to Samuel, "Do not look at his appearance or at his physical stature, because I have refused him. For the LORD does not see as man sees; for man looks at the outward appearance, but the LORD looks at the heart.
Mat 15:15-20 (verse 18), Mark 10:5-9 (verse 5)

Line: *Jesus said they do not know they are wretched, miserable, poor, blind and naked.*
Eccl 4:1-7 8 There is one alone, without companion: He has neither son nor brother. Yet *there is* no end to all his labors, Nor is his eye satisfied with riches. *But he never asks,* "For whom do I toil and deprive myself of good?" This also *is* vanity and a grave misfortune.
1 Tim 6:17-19 (verse 17)

Line: *Then Jesus goes on to tell them to buy gold from Him, that has been refined by fire.*
Pr 16:8-12 8 Better *is* a little with righteousness, Than vast revenues without justice.
Heb 13:1-6 (verses 5-6)

Line: *He wants them to have white garments so that they can clothe themselves.*
Rev 19:11-16 14 And the armies in heaven, clothed in fine linen, white and clean, followed Him on white horses.
Isa 1:17-20 (verse 18), John 8:1-12 (verse 12)

Line: *He wants them to have their eyes to be opened so that they can see.*
Pr 30:11-15 12 There is a generation that is pure in its own eyes, Yet is not washed from its filthiness. 13 There is a generation—oh, how lofty are their eyes! And their eyelids are lifted up.
Read Rev 3:18 notes from the NET BIBLE at bible.org

Line: *Because HE LOVES THEM, he reproves and disciplines them who have this spirit.*
Heb 12:5-11 5 And you have forgotten the exhortation which speaks to you as to sons: "My son, do not despise the chastening of the LORD, Nor be discouraged when you are rebuked by Him; 6 For whom the LORD loves He chastens, And scourges every son whom He receives."
I Cor 11:27-34 (verse 32)

Line: *Jesus is knocking on the door to their spirit, waiting for them to open their spirit to Him.*
Isa 54:1-16 5 For your Maker *is* your husband, The LORD of hosts *is* His name; And your Redeemer *is* the Holy One of Israel; He is called the God of the whole earth.

Subtitle: The Church Can Change Our Nations
Line: *The other thing He downloaded into me is "How the church down here on earth goes, so does a nation."*
2 Chron 6:1-42 34 When Your people go out to battle against their enemies, wherever You send them, and when they pray to You toward this city which You have chosen and the

temple which I have built for Your name, 35 then hear from heaven their prayer and their supplication, and maintain their cause.
Gen 41:1-57 (verse 28)

Line: *He really does want His people who are called by His name to humble themselves, pray, seek His face and turn from their individual wicked ways.*
2 Chron 7:12-22 14 if My people who are called by My name will humble themselves, and pray and seek My face, and turn from their wicked ways, then I will hear from heaven, and will forgive their sin and heal their land..
Gen 18:1-33 (verse 32), Dan 4:1-37 (verses 1-3)

Line: *This always turns a nation around.*
Jonah 3:1-10 5 So the people of Nineveh believed God, proclaimed a fast, and put on sackcloth, from the greatest to the least of them. 10 Then God saw their works, that they turned from their evil way; and God relented from the disaster that He had said He would bring upon them, and He did not do it.
2 Chron 20:1-30 (verses 3,15,27)

Line: *We that believe in Jesus as Lord and Savior, can change our nations around, whether it is the United States, Peru, France, England, Canada, China, Uganda, Israel, or your nation.*
1 Tim 2:1-7 1 Therefore I exhort first of all that supplications, prayers, intercessions, *and* giving of thanks be made for all men, 2 for kings and all who are in authority, that we may lead a quiet and peaceable life in all godliness and reverence. 3 For this *is* good and acceptable in the sight of God our Savior, 4 who desires all men to be saved and to come to the knowledge of the truth.

Chapter 14 Notes
What God Does With Our Prayers

Subtitle: 2 Corinthians 5:8 (NKJV) ...to be absent from the body and to be present with the Lord.

Line: *I knew where I was going.*

John 14:1-6 3 And if I go and prepare a place for you, I will come again and receive you to Myself; that where I am, *there* you may be also. 4 And where I go you know, and the way you know.

Phil 1:19-26 (verse 21)

Line: *As 2 Corinthians says, I was absent from my body, and was in the presence of my Lord.*

2 Cor 5:1-8 8 We are confident, yes, well pleased rather to be absent from the body and to be present with the Lord.

1 Cor 15:50-54 (verses 51-52)

Line: *Yet the prayers of people that were praying for me and other prayers were moving faster than I was.*

Dan 10:10-21 12 Then he said to me, "Do not fear, Daniel, for from the first day that you set your heart to understand, and to humble yourself before your God, your words were heard; and I have come because of your words.

1 John 5:14-15 (verse 14)

Subtitle: Two Types Of Prayers

Line: *One type were prayers from people that had prayed a prayer and understood the authority they had when they prayed the prayer.*

Mark 11:20-24 24 Therefore I say to you, whatever things you ask when you pray, believe that you receive them, and you will have them.

John 15:1-8 (verse 7), 1 John 5:14-15 (verse 14)

Line: *They were praying in faith from their hearts.*
Ps 34:1-22 18 The LORD *is* near to those who have a broken heart, And saves such as have a contrite spirit.

Line: *They were praying according to a verse in the Bible that they had understood the meaning of.*
Heb 4:8-13 12 For the word of God *is* living and powerful, and sharper than any two-edged sword, piercing even to the division of soul and spirit, and of joints and marrow, and is a discerner of the thoughts and intents of the heart.
Eph 1:15-22 (verse 17)

Line: *They were praying the will of God over me and others.*
Rom 8:18-30 26 Likewise the Spirit also helps in our weaknesses. For we do not know what we should pray for as we ought, but the Spirit Himself makes intercession for us with groanings which cannot be uttered. 27 Now He who searches the hearts knows what the mind of the Spirit is, because He makes intercession for the saints according to the will of God.
Mat 6:5-14 (verse 10), Mat 21:19-22 (verse 22)

Line: *And they knew that God would answer the prayer with His power.*
1 John 3:16-23 22 And whatever we ask we receive from Him, because we keep His commandments and do those things that are pleasing in His sight.
John 9:13-34 (verse 31)

Line: *We are told to pray His will here on earth in Matthew 6:10.*
Mat 6:5-14 9 In this manner, therefore, pray: Our Father in heaven, Hallowed be Your name. 10 Your kingdom come. Your will be done On earth as *it is* in heaven.
Luke 11:1-4 (verse 2)

Line: *But also remember my wife's sacrifice and battle to get that outcome.*
Luke 18:1-8 1 Then He spoke a parable to them, that men always ought to pray and not lose heart,
Ezek 22:23-30 (verse 30), Mat 7:7-12 (verse 7)

Line: *They had faith in what they prayed, not really understanding what they were fully praying for.*
Eph 3:14-21 20 Now to Him who is able to do exceedingly abundantly above all that we ask or think, according to the power that works in us
Gen 19:27-29 (verse 29)

Subtitle: Where Our Prayers Go
Line: *Not only did they go to the Father God, they went inside of Him.*
Rev 8:1-6 4 And the smoke of the incense, with the prayers of the saints, ascended before God from the angel's hand.
Ps 141:1-10 (verse 2), 2 Chron 30:1-27 (verse 27), Rev 5:1-10 (verse 8)

Line: *I came to understand that He answers our prayers with Himself.*
Luke 11:9-13 13 If you then, being evil, know how to give good gifts to your children, how much more will *your* heavenly Father give the Holy Spirit to those who ask Him!"
Ps 28:6-9, verse 7, Ps 46:1, verse 1, Ps 78:67-72, verse 72, Ps 118:25-27, verse 27, Pr 3:21-26, verse 26 2 Cor 1:3-7, verse 3

Subtitle: Prayers From The Heart
Line: *I understood our prayers must come from our heart.*
2 Chron 6:1-42 29 whatever prayer, whatever supplication is *made* by anyone, or by all Your people Israel, when each one knows his own burden and his own grief, and spreads

out his hands to this temple: 30 then hear from heaven Your dwelling place, and forgive, and give to everyone according to all his ways, whose heart You know (for You alone know the hearts of the sons of men)
Pr 23:1-35 (verse 12)

Line: *Our God is a heart God, and He is looking for us to talk to Him from our heart.*
Ps 66:16-20 18 If I regard iniquity in my heart, The Lord will not hear.
Dan 10:10-20 (verse 12)

Line: *I do not have the word yet to describe this, but our prayers become substances.*
Rev 5:1-10 8 Now when He had taken the scroll, the four living creatures and the twenty-four elders fell down before the Lamb, each having a harp, and golden bowls full of incense, which are the prayers of the saints.
Ps 141:1-10 (verse 2), Rev 8:1-6 (verses 3-4)

Line: *This is why most little children receive their request.*
Mat 18:1-5 4 Therefore whoever humbles himself as this little child is the greatest in the kingdom of heaven.
Mark 10:13-16 (verse 15)

Line: *He understands your heart.*
Ps 139:1-6 1 O LORD, You have searched me and known me.
Mark 2:1-2 (verse 8), Luke 6:43-45 (verse 45)

Line: *He only hears prayers from the heart.*
Acts 10:1-8 2 a devout man and one who feared God with all his household, who gave alms generously to the people, and prayed to God always. 4 And when he observed him, he was afraid, and said, "What is it, lord?" So he said to him,

"Your prayers and your alms have come up for a memorial before God.
Dan 10:10-20 (verse 12)

Line: *The Holy Spirit will let you know.*
John 16:5-15 13 However, when He, the Spirit of truth, has come, He will guide you into all truth; for He will not speak on His own *authority,* but whatever He hears He will speak; and He will tell you things to come.
John 14:15-18 (verse 17), Heb 10:11-17 (verse 15)

Line: *He will also help you to pray from your heart.*
Rom 8:18-30 26 Likewise the Spirit also helps in our weaknesses. For we do not know what we should pray for as we ought, but the Spirit Himself makes intercession for us with groanings which cannot be uttered. 27 Now He who searches the hearts knows what the mind of the Spirit is, because He makes intercession for the saints according to the will of God.

Line: *The Holy Spirit came to help us do a lot of things right; the way God wants them done.*
1 Cor 2:10-16 11 For what man knows the things of a man except the spirit of the man which is in him? Even so no one knows the things of God except the Spirit of God. 12 Now we have received, not the spirit of the world, but the Spirit who is from God, that we might know the things that have been freely given to us by God.
John 7:37-39 (verses 38-39) Jude 1:20-23 (verse 20)

Line: *My reply to them is, "Ask Him to help you pray from your heart."*
Ps 51:1-19 10 Create in me a clean heart, O God, And renew a steadfast spirit within me.

Line: *After you ask Him from your heart, you do not have to ask Him again.*

Mat 7:7-12 11 If you then, being evil, know how to give good gifts to your children, how much more will your Father who is in heaven give good things to those who ask Him!

Ps 50:12-15 (verse 15), Ps 66:19-20 (verses 19-20)

Line: *Now thank Him.*

Phil 4:2-7 6 Be anxious for nothing, but in everything by prayer and supplication, with thanksgiving, let your requests be made known to God;

Col 4:2-6 (verse 2)

Subtitle: Prayers Don't Have A Shelf Life

Line: Another thing I came to understand about prayer is that if it is a prayer from the heart, it does not have a shelf life.

John 17:20-26 20 "I do not pray for these alone, but also for those who will believe in Me through their word; 21 that they all may be one, as You, Father, *are* in Me, and I in You; that they also may be one in Us, that the world may believe that You sent Me.

Ps 102:12-22 (verse 17), Acts 10:1-8 (verse 4)

Line: *He wants your loved ones to be saved more than you do.*

John 3:1-21 17 For God did not send His Son into the world to condemn the world, but that the world through Him might be saved.

Line: *Remember, the Father gave his Son, Jesus, so that they could be saved.*

Rom 5:6-10 8 But God demonstrates His own love toward us, in that while we were still sinners, Christ died for us.

Line: *It does not matter if you see it answered here on earth or when you are in heaven.*
Luke 15:1-10 7 I say to you that likewise there will be more joy in heaven over one sinner who repents than over ninety-nine just persons who need no repentance. 10 Likewise, I say to you, there is joy in the presence of the angels of God over one sinner who repents.

Line: *They prayed for a great, great, great, great grandchild to know Jesus as Lord and Savior.*
1 Tim 1:13-7 5 when I call to remembrance the genuine faith that is in you, which dwelt first in your grandmother Lois and your mother Eunice, and I am persuaded is in you also.

Line: *Our prayers cause movement in the Kingdom of God. Jesus is strategizing by how we pray.*
Mat 9:35-38 38 Therefore pray the Lord of the harvest to send out laborers into His harvest.
Ex 34:1-10 (verse 9), Phil 1:19-26 (verse 19)

Line: *In the Bible we can read that we are to pray for the Lord to send laborers into His harvest in Matthew 9:37-38.*
Luke 10:1-12 22 Then He said to them, "The harvest truly is great, but the laborers are few; therefore pray the Lord of the harvest to send out laborers into His harvest.
Gen 19:1-29 (verse 29)

Subtitle: Jesus Giving Out Orders

Line: *Another thing that must be said loud and clear is that we have the only God who hears prayer.*
John 11:38-44 41 Then they took away the stone from the place where the dead man was lying. And Jesus lifted up His eyes and said, "Father, I thank You that You have heard Me. 42 And I know that You always hear Me, but because of the

people who are standing by I said this, that they may believe that You sent Me."
Ps 65:1-4 (verse 2), Ps 115:3-8 (verses 4-6)

Line: *I saw only one God, and He was not sharing His throne with anyone else.*
John 17:1-5 3 And this is eternal life, that they may know You, the only true God, and Jesus Christ whom You have sent.
1 King 18:1-39 (verse 27), Ps 68:1-35 (verse 20)

Chapter 15 Notes
I Saw God The Father On His Throne And His Love For Us!

Subtitle: None

Line: *He is the true Spirit and we must worship Him in spirit and truth.*

John 4:1-26 23 But the hour is coming, and now is, when the true worshipers will worship the Father in spirit and truth; for the Father is seeking such to worship Him. 24 God *is* Spirit, and those who worship Him must worship in spirit and truth."

Isa 40:27-31 (verse 28), Jer 23:16-24 (verse 24)

Line: *I heard all of creation, but those who have been redeemed refer to the Father God as the WORD.*

John 1:1-5 1 In the beginning was the Word, and the Word was with God, and the Word was God.

Ps 54:41, Ps 119:84-96 (verse 89)

Line: *Now, those of us who are redeemed would call Him Father.*

John 20:11-18 17 Jesus said to her, "Do not cling to Me, for I have not yet ascended to My Father; but go to My brethren and say to them, 'I am ascending to My Father and your Father, and *to* My God and your God.'"

John 1:6-13 (verse 12), Eph 5:1-6 (verse 1)

Subtitle: What Does The Father Look Like?

Line: *He is vast.*

Ps 90:1-2 2 Before the mountains were brought forth, Or ever You had formed the earth and the world, Even from everlasting to everlasting, You are God.

Job 9:1-35 (verses 10-11), Ps 89:5-7 (verse 6)

Line: *The angels that fly around him saying, "holy, holy, holy" to Him, are very small compared to God.*

Rev 4:1-8 8 The angels that fly around him saying, "holy, holy, holy" to Him, are very small compared to God. "Holy, holy, holy, Lord God Almighty, Who was and is and is to come!"

Line: *Or better yet, we have the form of God.*

Gen 1:24-28 26 Then God said, "Let Us make man in Our image, according to Our likeness; let them have dominion over the fish of the sea, over the birds of the air, and over the cattle, over all the earth and over every creeping thing that creeps on the earth."

Num 23:19, 1 Sam 15:24-35 (verse 29), Rom 1:18-32 (verse 25)

Line: *He is bright like Jesus with many colors coming off of Him.*

Dan 7:7-10 9 "I watched till thrones were put in place, And the Ancient of Days was seated; His garment *was* white as snow, And the hair of His head *was* like pure wool. His throne *was* a fiery flame, Its wheels a burning fire;

Deut 33:1-2 (verse 2), Ps 18:7-15 (verse 12)

Subtitle: The Father's Throne

Line: *He was siting on the throne and He is the throne.*

Ps 45:1-17 6 Your throne, O God, *is* forever and ever; A scepter of righteousness *is* the scepter of Your kingdom.

Rev 20:11-15 (verse 11)

Line: *The throne was bright and looked like a cloud.*

Ex 34:1-9 5 Now the LORD descended in the cloud and stood with him there, and proclaimed the name of the LORD. 6 And the LORD passed before him and proclaimed, "The LORD,

the LORD God, merciful and gracious, longsuffering, and abounding in goodness and truth,
Ps 68:1-35 (verses 4,33-34), 2 Chro 6:1-11 (verse 1)

Line: *What I experienced about the throne was that God the Father was and has never been separated from the throne.*
Luke 9:27-36 34 While he was saying this, a cloud came and overshadowed them; and they were fearful as they entered the cloud. 35 And a voice came out of the cloud, saying, "This is My beloved Son. Hear Him!
Ex 13:21-22, Rev 15:5-8 (verse 8)

Line: *I only could say to myself after seeing God on the throne, in the midst of the throne, and being the throne, "Who could make a throne for God, but God?"*
Ps 90:1-2 2 Before the mountains were brought forth, Or ever You had formed the earth and the world, Even from everlasting to everlasting, You *are* God.
Ps 50:12-15 (verse 12), Ps 68:32-35 (verse 35), Dan 7:11-14 (verse 13)

Subtitle: Our Father's Love For Us
Line: *But out of all that I saw, what really stood out to me was the love that He has for each and every one of us on earth.*
Eph 1:3-6 3 Blessed *be* the God and Father of our Lord Jesus Christ, who has blessed us with every spiritual blessing in the heavenly *places* in Christ, 4 just as He chose us in Him before the foundation of the world, that we should be holy and without blame before Him in love,
Ps 36:6-5 (verse 5), 1 John 4:7-10 (verse 10)

Line: *I came to understand that every time we take a breath of air, the Father God is saying, "I love you."*

Gen 2:1-7 7 And the LORD God formed man *of* the dust of the ground, and breathed into his nostrils the breath of life; and man became a living being.

Subtitle: We Are All Number One

Line: *I understood that there is no number two in God's eyes.*

1 John 3:1-3 1 Behold what manner of love the Father has bestowed on us, that we should be called children of God! Therefore the world does not know us, because it did not know Him.

Ps 36:7-9 (verse 7), John 15:9-16 (verse 9)

Line: *I came to know how valuable we are to Him:*

Mat 10:27-31 29 Are not two sparrows sold for a copper coin? And not one of them falls to the ground apart from your Father's will. 30 But the very hairs of your head are all numbered. 31 Do not fear therefore; you are of more value than many sparrows.

Ps 33:10-12 (verse 12), Col 1:12-14 (verse 13), Rom 8:29-33 (verse 31)

Chapter 16 Notes
Worship Before The Throne Of God

Subtitle: None

Line: *Between them and the throne was something like water. John said in Revelations that it was like a crystal sea.*
Rev 4:1-11 6 Before the throne there was a sea of glass, like crystal. And in the midst of the throne, and around the throne, were four living creatures full of eyes in front and in back.
Rev 15:1-3 (verse 2)

Line: *Just before I saw what was happening before the throne of God, all of what we would call sound, stopped.*
Rev 8:1-6 1 When He opened the seventh seal, there was silence in heaven for about half an hour.
Zech 2 :6-13 (verse 13)

Subtitle: The Heavenly Worship Leader

Line: *This being seemed to be making music within itself.*
Ezek 28:14-13 13 You were in Eden, the garden of God; Every precious stone *was* your covering: The sardius, topaz, and diamond, Beryl, onyx, and jasper, Sapphire, turquoise, and emerald with gold. The workmanship of your timbrels and pipes.

Subtitle: A Call To Worship

Line: *It was calling all of heaven to praise the Father and Jesus, which was this being's purpose.*
Ps 66:1-20 1 Make a joyful shout to God, all the earth! 2 Sing out the honor of His name; Make His praise glorious.
Ps 108:1-6 (verse 2)

Line: *For I saw to the right of me and to the right of the throne, a large multitude of beings came up as on a number of elevators off of their knees like the first being did.*

Dan 7:9-17 10 A fiery stream issued And came forth from before Him. A thousand thousands ministered to Him; Ten thousand times ten thousand stood before Him. The court was seated, And the books were opened.
Rev 7:9-13 (verse 9), Rev 19:1-7 (verses 1,6)

Subtitle: The Multitude Of Beings

Line: *I knew that some of the heavenly beings had been there before the throne for what seemed to me, to be forever.*
Rev 4:7-11 8 The four living creatures, each having six wings, were full of eyes around and within. And they do not rest day or night, saying: "Holy, holy, holy, Lord God Almighty, Who was and is and is to come!"
1 Chron 16:7-36 (verse 36), Ps 90:1-2 (verse 2)

Line: *Each being was shining and beautiful. All the redeemed (who had been human on earth) where shining and white as light, the others were all colors and shining.*
Dan 12:1-3 3 Those who are wise shall shine Like the brightness of the firmament, And those who turn many to righteousness Like the stars forever and ever.
Rev 19:11-16 (verse 14), Mark 9:1-12 (verse 3)

Line: *They started to praise the Father.*
Rev 5:8-14 9 And they sang a new song, saying: "You are worthy to take the scroll, And to open its seals;
For You were slain, And have redeemed us to God by Your blood Out of every tribe and tongue and people and nation, 11 Then I looked, and I heard the voice of many angels around the throne, the living creatures, and the elders; and the number of them was ten thousand times ten thousand, and thousands of thousands.
Ps 117:1-2 (verse 1), Rev 4:10-11 (verse 11)

Line: *Each song sounded so wonderful, beautiful, lovely, and words I have not put a voice to.*
Rev 14:1-5 3 They sang as it were a new song before the throne, before the four living creatures, and the elders; and no one could learn that song except the hundred *and* forty-four thousand who were redeemed from the earth.

Subtitle: The Crystal-Like Sea's Part In Worship

Line: *Before they got to the Father, the Crystal-like Sea that was before the throne rose up in the atmosphere and intercepted the notes and would make a hole in itself to have the notes dance through.*
Ps 93:1-4 3 The floods have lifted up, O LORD, The floods have lifted up their voice; The floods lift up their waves. 4 The LORD on high is mightier Than the noise of many waters, Than the mighty waves of the sea.
Rev 22:1-5 (verse 1)

Subtitle: Dancing In Heaven

Line: *After the notes left the Crystal-like Sea into the atmosphere, the notes met up with the colors coming off of the Father.*
Ezek 1:1-28 28 Like the appearance of a rainbow in a cloud on a rainy day, so *was* the appearance of the brightness all around it. This *was* the appearance of the likeness of the glory of the LORD.
Rev 4:1-11 (verse 3)

Subtitle: The Thunders Of Heaven

Line: *The atmospheres were praising the Father on the throne.*
Rev 10:1-7 4 Now when the seven thunders uttered their voices, I was about to write; but I heard a voice from heaven saying to me, "Seal up the things which the seven thunders uttered, and do not write them."

Ps 65:7-9 (verse 8), Ps 89:5-10 (verse 5), Rev 4:1-11 (verse 5), Rev 14:1-5 (verse 2)

Subtitle: The Beings Flying Around The Father
Line: *Living Creatures as John said in Revelations 4:6-7, 9 and seraphim as Isaiah called them in Isaiah 6:2-4.*
Rev 4:6-7 9 Whenever the living creatures give glory and honor and thanks to Him who sits on the throne, who lives forever and ever,
Isa 6:2-4 (verse 2)

Line: *Some had what looked like eyes on their wings and others did not.*
Rev 4:6-8 8 The four living creatures, each having six wings, were full of eyes around and within. And they do not rest day or night, saying: "Holy, holy, holy, Lord God Almighty, Who was and is and is to come!"

Line: *Within His glory, is His praise for Himself.*
Ps 24:1-10 8 Who *is* this King of glory? The LORD strong and mighty, The LORD mighty in battle. 10 Who is this King of glory? The LORD of hosts, He *is* the King of glory. Selah
Ex 3:13-22 (verse 14), Ps 8:1, 2 Cor 1:15-24 (verse 20), Rev 4:1-8 (verse 3)

Subtitle: The Father's Love Song
Line: *This sound was God the Father singing back to each and every being giving Him praise before the throne.*
Zeph 3:14-20 17 The LORD your God in your midst, The Mighty One, will save; He will rejoice over you with gladness, He will quiet *you* with His love, He will rejoice over you with singing."
Job 35:10, Ps 68:33

Line: *Nothing in heaven stopped it or would think to stopping the song from reaching the targeted being.*
Ps 93:1-5 4 The LORD on high is mightier Than the noise of many waters, Than the mighty waves of the sea

Subtitle: His Love Song For Us Only
Line: *All the time love from God is being sent out to each and every person and nothing can stop this love from reaching us.*
John 3:1-21 16 For God so loved the world that He gave His only begotten Son, that whoever believes in Him should not perish but have everlasting life.
Ps 33:13-15 (verse 15)

Line: We *can deny His love, reject His love or act like His love is not there, but He keeps sending it to us.*
John 3:1-21 17 For God did not send His Son into the world to condemn the world, but that the world through Him might be saved.

Chapter 17 Notes
God's Creation of Beings

Subtitle: None

Line: *There are those who had been humans here on earth and now are among the redeemed in heaven.*

Col 1:9-12 12 giving thanks to the Father who has qualified us to be partakers of the inheritance of the saints in the light.

Heb 12:18-24 (verse 23)

Line: *These beings had been on earth and had made Jesus their Lord and Savior while living on this earth.*

Heb 12:18-24 23 to the general assembly and church of the firstborn *who are* registered in heaven, to God the Judge of all, to the spirits of just men made perfect.

Gal 3:26-28 (verse 26)

Line: *They are perfect in every way, just as the Father, Jesus and Holy Spirit are perfect.*

Col 1:24-29 28 Him we preach, warning every man and teaching every man in all wisdom, that we may present every man perfect in Christ Jesus.

Heb 6:1-8 (verse 1), Jam 3:2-8 (verse 4)

Line: *They are right just like everything around them is right.*

Luke 9:27-36 29 As He prayed, the appearance of His face was altered, and His robe became white and glistening. 30 And behold, two men talked with Him, who were Moses and Elijah, 31 who appeared in glory and spoke of His decease which He was about to accomplish at Jerusalem.

Ezek 3:1-27 (verse 14), 1 Peter 5:1-5 (verse 4)

Line: *I saw life created.*
Col 1:16 For by Him all things were created that are in heaven and that are on earth, visible and invisible, whether thrones or dominions or principalities or powers. All things were created through Him and for Him.

Subtitle: My Family And Friends Welcome Me
Line: *I saw my Grandmother Mary, Grandfather Lewis, Grandmother Ruth, Grandfather Begron, and many of my parents' brothers and sisters.*
Mat 17:1-13 2 and He was transfigured before them. His face shone like the sun, and His clothes became as white as the light. 3 And behold, Moses and Elijah appeared to them, talking with Him.
Mat 27:45-56 (verses 52-53), Luke 16:19-31 (verse 23)

Line: *Every family member whom I was connected with because of the DNA inside of me was there; the DNA that God had made me out of.*
2 Tim 1:3-7 5 when I call to remembrance the genuine faith that is in you, which dwelt first in your grandmother Lois and your mother Eunice, and I am persuaded is in you also.
Ps 102:23-28 (verse 28), Ps 112:1-8 (verses 1-2)

Subtitle: Family Matters In Heaven
Line: *My family members and friends had pure love for me.*
1 John 3:1-3 3 And everyone who has this hope in Him purifies himself, just as He is pure.

Line: *This desire they had for me to be with them is the same desire we have for our love ones to live with us on earth forever.*
Rom 9:1-5 3 For I could wish that I myself were accursed from Christ for my brethren, my countrymen according to the flesh, 4 who are Israelites, to whom pertain the adoption,

the glory, the covenants, the giving of the law, the service of God, and the promises.

Line: *I understood that they do not want to come back here to be on earth.*
Rev 19:1-10 6 And I heard, as it were, the voice of a great multitude, as the sound of many waters and as the sound of mighty thunderings, saying, "Alleluia! For the Lord God Omnipotent reigns!

Line: *We were never meant to be apart. That was not in God's plans for us.*
Gen 2:1-25 24 Therefore a man shall leave his father and mother and be joined to his wife, and they shall become one flesh.

Subtitle: Bring Back As Many As You Can!

Line: *Jesus has sent us to our own family first. He wants us to talk to, and to be praying for them.*
Ps 103:15-18 17 But the mercy of the LORD *is* from everlasting to everlasting On those who fear Him, And His righteousness to children's children.
John 1:35-42 (verse 42)

Subtitle: What People Looked Like

Line: *My family members in heaven and others who had been human beings here on earth, **were shining** and had pure joy.*
Rev 19:11-21 14 And the armies in heaven, clothed in fine linen, white and clean, followed Him on white horses.
Isa 1:18-20 (verse 18), Isa 62:1-5 (verse 1)

Line: *My family members in heaven and others who had been human beings here on earth, were shining **and had pure joy.***

John 15:9-17 11 Now I am no longer in the world, but these are in the world, and I come to You. Holy Father, keep through Your name those whom You have given Me, that they may be one as We are.
Ps 92:1-4 (verse 4), Jude 1:24-25 (verse 24), Rev 6:7-17 (verse 11)

Line: *It is Jesus' brightness shining out of them that makes it look like a robe.*
Rev 21:22-27 23 The city had no need of the sun or of the moon to shine in it, for the glory of God illuminated it. The Lamb *is* its light. 24 And the nations of those who are saved shall walk in its light, and the kings of the earth bring their glory and honor into it.
Rev 7:9-17 (verse 9)

Subtitle: Are Children There?
Line: *They did not age because there is no time in heaven.*
John 3:1-21 16 For God so loved the world that He gave His only begotten Son, that whoever believes in Him should not perish but have everlasting life.
Mat 22:23-33 (verse 30), Mark 12:18-27 (verse 25), John 6:22-40 (verse 40)

Subtitle: What Will We Be Doing In Heaven?
Line: *Since you are there forever, you are fulfilling your purpose in heaven.*
Mat 17:1-12 17 And behold, Moses and Elijah appeared to them, talking with Him.
Rev 22:6-11 (verse 9)

Line: *No one was thinking that their purpose was any less than anyone else's purpose.*

1 Cor 12:12-31 12 For as the body is one and has many members, but all the members of that one body, being many, are one body, so also *is* Christ.

Line: *Every creation of God was serving each other.*
Isa 12:12-31 25 that there should be no schism in the body, but *that* the members should have the same care for one another.

Line: *Every creation was equal.*
Rom 12:3-8 5 of whom are the fathers and from whom, according to the flesh, Christ came, who is over all, the eternally blessed God. Amen.

Chapter 18 Notes
This Is Not Our Home

Subtitle: We Are Just Passing Through
Line: *It was great to really know that this was not my home.*

John 15:18-25 19 If you were of the world, the world would love its own. Yet because you are not of the world, but I chose you out of the world, therefore the world hates you.

2 Cor 4:18-5 (verse 18), 1 John 2:15-17 (verse 15)

Subtitle: This Earth Is Not Our Home
Line: *We are ambassadors here, we who know Jesus as Lord and Savior.*

2 Cor 5:12-21 20 Now then, we are ambassadors for Christ, as though God were pleading through us: we implore *you* on Christ's behalf, be reconciled to God.

Eph 6:10-20 (verse 20)

Line: *Today's earth is not as good as yesterday's earth and tomorrow's earth is not as good as today's.*

1 John 2:15-19 17 And the world is passing away, and the lust of it; but he who does the will of God abides forever.

Gen 3:17-19 (verses 17-18), Rom 8:20-22 (verse 21)

Line: *This is a desire of all of God's creation. This is the only desire of our Savior to all of mankind.*

Rom 8:18-30 22 For we know that the whole creation groans and labors with birth pangs together until now. 23 Not only *that,* but we also who have the firstfruits of the Spirit, even we ourselves groan within ourselves, eagerly waiting for the adoption, the redemption of our body.

Line: *God Himself, wants us to know this is not our home and we are only passing through.*

John 15:18-25 18 "If the world hates you, you know that it hated Me before *it hated* you. 19 If you were of the world, the world would love its own. Yet because you are not of the world, but I chose you out of the world, therefore the world hates you.
John 18:28-38 (verse 36), 1 John 2:15-17 (verse 15)

Line: *We will outlast every problem we have.*
Col 3:1-11 1 If then you were raised with Christ, seek those things which are above, where Christ is, sitting at the right hand of God.

Line: *We will live on either in heaven with God, or in hell where everything is wrong, but we are going to have to leave.*
Phil 3:17-21 19 whose end *is* destruction, whose god *is their* belly, and *whose* glory *is* in their shame — who set their mind on earthly things. 20 For our citizenship is in heaven, from which we also eagerly wait for the Savior, the Lord Jesus Christ.
John 6:22-40 (verse 40), 2 Thess 1:3-12 (verse 9)

Subtitle: The Elderly Lady
Line: *I was home. I was home. I WAS HOME!*
Eph 2:1-9 6 and raised *us* up together, and made *us* sit together in the heavenly *places* in Christ Jesus,
John 14:1-4 (verse 3)

Chapter 19 Notes
Angels

Subtitle: None

Line: *We as humans like to make gods out of God creations and angels are one of them.*

Rom 1:18-32 25 who exchanged the truth of God for the lie, and worshiped and served the creature rather than the Creator, who is blessed forever. Amen.

Gal 1:18-24 (verse 18), Col 2:11-23 (verse 18)

Line: *Humans like to make gods out of evil spirits, devils and demons.*

Rev 9:19-21 20 But the rest of mankind, who were not killed by these plagues, did not repent of the works of their hands, that they should not **worship demons**, and idols of gold, silver, brass, stone, and wood, which can neither see nor hear nor walk.

Jer 10:1-6 (verses 8-9), Hos 13:1-3 (verse 2)

Line: *They are made for His purpose.*

Ps 89:1-52 7 God is greatly to be feared in the assembly of the saints (Angels), And to be held in reverence by all *those* around Him.

Mat 26,47-56 (verse 53), Mat 28:1-8 (verses 2,7)

Line: *Now that you have these meanings let us look at these verses to understand that angels come in every size and shape. Some look like humans and some do not.*

Rev 4:6-9 7 The first living creature *was* like a lion, the second living creature like a calf, the third living creature had a face like a man, and the fourth living creature *was* like a flying eagle.

Ezek 1:1-28 (verse 10)

Subtitle: The House-Like Angels

Line: *There were so many horses. It was surprising to me..*
Zech 1:7-10 8 I saw by night, and behold, a man riding on a red horse, and it stood among the myrtle trees in the hollow; and behind him *were* horses: red, sorrel, and white.
Rev 6:1-9 (verses 2,4-5,8), Rev 19:11-21 (verses 11,14,18- 19,21)

Line: *And yet when you read the Bible you see in Revelation where Jesus is coming back on a white horse.*
Rev 19:110-12 11 Now I saw heaven opened, and behold, a white horse. And He who sat on him *was* called Faithful and True, and in righteousness He judges and makes war. 12 His eyes *were* like a flame of fire, and on His head *were* many crowns. He had a name written that no one knew except Himself.

Line: *There are also a red, a black, and a pail horse mentioned.*
Rev 6:1-17 2 And I looked, and behold, a white horse... 4 Another horse, fiery red, went out... 5 So I looked, and behold, a black horse... 8 So I looked, and behold, a pale horse...

Subtitle: The Little Angels

Line: *The smaller angels have just as much power as the bigger angels do because they are working under the authority of God. It is God that gives them power.*
Mat 13:34-52 41 The Son of Man will send out His angels, and they will gather out of His kingdom all things that offend, and those who practice lawlessness.
Mat 13:34-52 (verses 49-50)

Subtitle: Do We Have Guardian Angles?

Line: *One of the most asked questions I get is, "Do we have Guardian Angels? The answer is yes.*

Mat 18:10-14 10 Take heed that you do not despise one of these little ones, for I say to you that in heaven their angels always see the face of My Father who is in heaven.

Heb 1:3-14 (verse 14)

Line: *They are all doing what they are created to do for God in heaven with love.*

Ps 103:20-22 20 Bless the LORD, you His angels, Who excel in strength, who do His word, Heeding the voice of His word.

Dan 7:9-10 (verse 10)

Line: *We have more than one.*

2 Kings 6:8-23 17 And Elisha prayed, and said, "LORD, I pray, open his eyes that he may see." Then the LORD opened the eyes of the young man, and he saw. And behold, the mountain was full of horses and chariots of fire all around Elisha.

Subtitle: What Do Angels Look Like?

Line: *Maybe one out of four angels looked human.*

Ezek 1:1-28 10 As for the likeness of their faces, *each* had the face of a man; each of the four had the face of a lion on the right side, each of the four had the face of an ox on the left side, and each of the four had the face of an eagle.

Rev 4:1-11 (verse 7)

Line: *Angels are genderless; they only look like male or female.*

Mat 22:23-32 30 For in the resurrection they neither marry nor are given in marriage, but are like angels of God in heaven.

Mark 12:24-26 (verse 25), Luke 20:35-37 (verses 35-36)

Line: *There are angels that look like **light**, fire, water, air, clouds, wind, trees, and flowers.*
Luke 24:1-8 4 And it happened, as they were greatly perplexed about this, that behold, two men stood by them in shining garments.

Line: *There are angels that look like light, **fire,** water, air, clouds, wind, trees, and flowers.*
Heb 1:5-14 7 And of the angels He says: "Who makes His angels spirits And His ministers a flame of fire.
2 King 2:2-18 (verse 11)
Isa 6:1-3 (verse 2) seraphim means: burning one

Line: *So just know that there are more angels that stayed with God (Father, Son, Holy Spirit) than went with Satan.*
Rev 12:7-12 9 So the great dragon was cast out, that serpent of old, called the Devil and Satan, who deceives the whole world; he was cast to the earth, and his angels were cast out with him.

Line: *I end this chapter with this - we are only to worship God (Father, Son, Holy Spirit), and not angels.*
Rev 5:1-14 11 Then I looked, and I heard the voice of many angels around the throne, the living creatures, and the elders; and the number of them was ten thousand times ten thousand, and thousands of thousands, 12 saying with a loud voice: "Worthy is the Lamb who was slain To receive power and riches and wisdom, And strength and honor and glory and blessing!"

Chapter 20 Notes
Eight Things I Was Told About
The End Of The Age

Subtitle: THESE EIGHT THINGS WILL TAKE PLACE TO SIGNAL THE END OF THE AGE!

Line: *EVERY NATION IS HERE FOR THE PURPOSE OF GOD!*
Job 12:23-25 23 He makes nations great, and destroys them; He enlarges nations, and guides them.
Dan 4:13-18 (verse 17), Dan 4:23-25 (verse 25)

Line: *KINGS AND QUEENS, OR WHAT YOU CALL PRESIDENTS AND PRIME MINISTERS, ARE ALL PUT IN POWER FOR THE PURPOSE OF GOD!*
Rev 17:12-18 17 For God has put it into their hearts to fulfill His purpose, to be of one mind, and to give their kingdom to the beast, until the words of God are fulfilled.
Dan 2:20-23 (verse 21)

Line: *MORE, EVERYDAY, SONS AND DAUGHTERS OF GOD WILL BE PLACED IN RULERSHIP OF NATIONS FOR THE PURPOSE OF GOD!*
Job 36:7 He does not withdraw His eyes from the righteous; But *they are* on the throne with kings, For He has seated them forever, And they are exalted.
Job 34:29-30 (verse 30)

Line: *RAISING PEOPLE FROM THE DEAD WILL BE COMMON IN THE LAST DAYS OF THE AGE!*
Luke 7:11-17 14 Then He came and touched the open coffin, and those who carried *him* stood still. And He said, "Young man, I say to you, arise." 15 So he who was dead sat up and began to speak. And He presented him to his mother.
Mat 9:18-26 (verses 24-25), John 11:1-44 (verses 43-44)

Line: *GOD IS NOT WORKING THROUGH ONE PERSON, BUT THROUGH HIS SONS AND DAUGHTERS IN THE PRESENT AGE. STOP PEOPLE FROM CHASING MEN, BUT HAVE THEM FOLLOW GOD!*
Titus 1:10-16 10 For there are many insubordinate, both idle talkers and deceivers, especially those of the circumcision, 11 whose mouths must be stopped, who subvert whole households, teaching things which they ought not, for the sake of dishonest gain.

Line: *THE GOOD NEWS OF GOD IS NOT FOR SALE AND HE IS GOING TO STOP THE SELLING OF IT BY HAVING MORE GIVE WHAT THEY KNOW AWAY. FREELY IT HAS BEEN GIVEN AND FREELY THEY MUST GIVE!*
Mat 10:5-15 8 Heal the sick, cleanse the lepers, raise the dead, cast out demons. Freely you have received, freely give. 9 Provide neither gold nor silver nor copper in your money belts.
Jer 23:1-8 (verse 2), 1 Tim 6:3-10 (verse 3)

Line: *THAT WHICH IS EVIL WILL LOOK GOOD, EVEN TO THE SONS AND DAUGHTERS OF GOD. THE SONS AND DAUGHTERS OF GOD WILL GROW IN PRAYER IN THAT TIME AND NEW EYES WILL OPEN, SPIRITUAL EYES. THEY WILL SEE FROM THE HEART!*
Mark 13:3-13 5 And Jesus, answering them, began to say: "Take heed that no one deceives you. 6 For many will come in My name, saying, 'I am He,' and will deceive many.
Isa 30:8-11-13 (verse 10), Eph 1:15-21 (verse 18)

Line: *VISUAL DECEPTION WILL INCREASE IN ALL AREAS OF THE WORLD!*
2 Thess 2:1-11 9 The coming of the *lawless one* is according to the working of Satan, with all power, signs, and lying wonders, 10 and with all unrighteous deception among those

who perish, because they did not receive the love of the truth, that they might be saved.
Mat 6:22-23 (verse 22), Heb 3:7-15 (verse 13)